VOGUE® KNITTING

accessorize™

scarves · hats · ponchos · socks & mittens

VOGUE® KNITTING
accessorize™

scarves · hats · ponchos · socks & mittens

sixth&spring books

Sixth&Spring Books

233 Spring Street

New York, New York 10013

Editorial Director
Trisha Malcolm

Art Director
Chi Ling Moy

Book Editor
Miriam Gold

Technical Editor
Carla Scott

Copy Editor
Pat Harste

Production Designer
Christy Hale

Yarn Editor
Veronica Manno

Manager, Book Division
Michelle Lo

Production Manager
David Joinnides

President and Publisher, Sixth&Spring Books
Art Joinnides

1 3 5 7 9 10 8 6 4 2

Library of Congress Cataloging-in-Publication Data

Vogue knitting accessorize: scarves, hats, ponchos, socks & mittens.

p cm.

ISBN 1-931543-57-7

1. Knitting--Patterns. 2. Hats. 3. Scarves. 4. Shawls. 5. Socks. I. Vogue knitting international.

TT825.V575 2004

746.43'20432--dc22

2003067342

Manufactured in China

Photo credits:

Paul Amato
2, 5, 7, 9, 13, 19, 21, 25, 31, 35, 37, 41, 43, 45, 47, 49, 51, 53, 55, 59, 63, 69,
71, 73, 77, 83, 87, 89, 91, 93, 95, 111, 115, 120, 121, 123, 125, 126, 127, 128,
130, 131, 131, 132, 133, 135, 136, 138, 141, 143, 144, 145, 146, 149

Enrique Cubillo
113, 157

William Garrett
79, 140

Jim Jordan
Front cover, 11, 17, 23, 29, 33. 57, 67, 97, 99, 103, 105, 118, 119, 124, 125,
132, 134, 146, 153, 154, 158

Brian Kraus
111, 155

Francis Milon
39

Rudy Molacek
75, 85, 137, 142

Eugene Mozgalevsky for Jack Deutsch Studio
81, 109, 141, 154

Dick Nystrom
15, 119

Richard Pierce
107, 154

Peggy Sirota
61, 65, 134

Nick Vaccaro
27, 124

contents

introduction

Why a book of accessories? Why not a book of chunky pullovers, cool tank tops or intricate cardigans? After all, it does seem that much of the time we spend knitting, we spend on projects of this kind—beautiful, cozy, and most importantly, practical. While practicality is part of the craft, and is certainly part of its appeal, there is a whole other world out there to enjoy, a place where uniqueness and originality rule, and where it's all about style.

Welcome to the world of accessories, where without jewelry, purses, hats, shoes or scarves, even the most modish of outfits will fall flat. That's where this collection comes in; filled with dozens of designs, you will find amazing accessories that will add flair, élan and excitement to any look.

The effect will be even more fantastic because the marriage of knitting and accessories is such a natural one. Both offer a one-of-a-kind quality, giving you the opportunity to wear something you've created with your own two hands. It is with this spirit in mind that we've given you these wonderful patterns with which to work. We encourage you to go farther than we have, to experiment: try different colors and yarns, see what new textures you can achieve and what unique fashions you can create. What may seem like a casual accessory in one form could be transformed into something extraordinary with only the slightest change.

We're pleased to offer you this fabulously chic collection. Hours were spent poring over hundreds of our patterns, choosing the most stylish and dynamic from our past issues. Our diverse assortment includes down-home socks; dramatic wraps; trendy ponchos; beautiful scarves and hats; and lovely purses—in short, any kind of accessory for every kind of outfit. Now it's up to you to make them your own.

under wraps

18¾/45.5cm wide by 54"/137cm long (length is measured from inside joining point of back neck).

MATERIALS

• 6 1¾oz/50g balls (each approx 148yd/136m) of Dale of Norway *Sisik* (wool/mohair/acrylic/viscose ③) in #160 olive tweed (MC)

• 2 1¾oz/50g balls (each approx 126yd/116m) of Dale of Norway *Tiur* (mohair/wool ③) each in #9853 olive (A), #2343 khaki (B) and #9835 lt olive (C)

• One pair size 5 (3.75mm) needles OR SIZE TO OBTAIN GAUGE

• Size 5 (3.75mm) circular needle, 29"/74cm long

GAUGE

18 sts and 25 rows = 4"/10cm over pat st (after blocking) using size 5 (3.75mm) needles.

TAKE TIME TO CHECK GAUGE.

Note: When changing colors in pat st, carry MC along sides of rows. Cut colors A, B and C and rejoin at each color stripe.

LONG RECTANGLE

With straight needles and MC, cast on 81 sts. Work the next 3 preparation rows as foll: **Preparation row 1 (WS)** Purl. **Preparation row 2 (RS)** Knit. **Preparation row 3 (WS)** P2, *wrapping yarn around needle twice, p1, then p3; rep from * ending last rep p2 instead of p3.

Beg pat st

Row 1 (RS) With A, k2, *sl 1 st wyib, then dropping the extra wrap, k1 st, insert RH needle into the next st 2 rows below and pull up a loop loosely, k the next st, pass the loop over the st just knit, k1; rep from *, end sl 1 wyib, k2. **Row 2** With

designed by barbara venishnick

(Continued on page 118)

wide rib shrug

very easy very vogue

SIZES

To fit Small/Medium (Large/X-Large). Shown in size Small/Medium.

KNITTED MEASUREMENTS

• Width (slightly stretched) approx 36 (41½)"/91.5 (105.5)cm

• Length (folded) 10 (11)"/25.5 (28)cm

MATERIALS

• 4 (5) 3½oz/100g balls (each approx 60yd/55m) of Tahki Yarns/Tahki•Stacy Charles, Inc., *Baby* (wool ⑥) in #18 brown

• Size 13 (9mm) circular needle, 24"/60cm or 32"/80cm long OR SIZE TO OBTAIN GAUGE

• St marker

GAUGE

10 sts and 13 rnds = 4"/10cm over k4, p4 rib (slightly stretched) using size 13 (9mm) needles.

TAKE TIME TO CHECK GAUGE.

Notes: 1) If necessary, to make edges looser, use one size larger needle to cast on and bind off. 2) To make shrug wider or narrower, simply add or subtract 8 sts to cast-on. Be sure to adjust yarn amounts if changing dimensions.

SHRUG

Cast on 88 (104) sts. Join, taking care not to twist sts on needle. Place a marker for end of rnd and slip marker every rnd.

Rnd 1 *K4, p4; rep from * around. Rep rnd 1 for rib until piece measures 14 (15)"/35.5 (38)cm from beg, or 4"/10cm less than desired length. Bind off loosely in rib.

FINISHING

Fold 4"/10cm from bound-off edge to RS.

designed by rosemary drysdale

- 11 1¾oz/50g skeins (each approx 100yd/92m) Plymouth Yarns *Indiecita Alpaca Worsted Weight* (alpaca ③) in #208 camel (MC)
- 1 skein in #500 black (CC)
- Size 7 (4.5mm) circular needle 24"/61cm long OR SIZE NEEDED TO OBTAIN GAUGE
- Size G (4.5mm) crochet hook

GAUGE

18 sts and 24 rows = 4"/10cm in St st (check gauge in St st as pat st falls into pleats) using size 7(4.5mm) needles.

TAKE TIME TO CHECK GAUGE.

Note: Always start a new skein of yarn at beg of row.

STITCH GLOSSARY

Bobble

K1, p1, k1, p1, k1 in one st, turn. Work 7 rows Garter st over 5 sts. **Next row** Sl 3 sts knitwise, k3tog tbl, place st on LH needle, k3tog, place st on LH needle. Insert RH needle into base of bobble (original first st), psso st on LH needle.

FLUTED RIB (multiple of 8 sts plus 1)

Rows 1-3 P1, *k1, p1; rep from *. **Row 4** Change to MC, K2, *p5, k3; rep from *, end p5, k2. **Row 5** P3, *k3, p5; rep

designed by linda cyr

trellis lace scarf

intermediate

SIZES

One size fits all.

KNITTED MEASUREMENTS

Approx 18" x 80"/45.5cm x 203cm

MATERIALS

• 5 .70oz/20g balls (each approx 325yd/300m) of Artisan NZ/Cherry Tree Hill, Inc., *Merino Lace Weight* (wool ①) in #F01 white

• One pair size 2 (2.5mm) needles OR SIZE TO OBTAIN GAUGE

• Two size 2 (2.5mm) dpn

• Stitch holder

GAUGE

36 sts and 44 rows = 4"/10cm over St st using size 2 (2.5mm) needles.

TAKE TIME TO CHECK GAUGE.

TRELLIS PATTERN (multiple of 15 sts plus 4)

Row 1 K4, *[yo, ssk] twice, yo, sl 2, k1, p2sso, [yo, k2tog] twice, yo, k1, p2, k1; rep from * to last 15 sts, [yo, ssk] twice, yo, sl 2, k1, p2sso, [yo, k2tog] twice, yo, k4. **Rows 2 and 4** K3, *p13, k2; rep from * to last 16 sts, p13, k3. **Row 3** K3, *[yo, ssk] 3 times, k1, [k2tog, yo] 3 times, p2; rep from * to last 16 sts, [yo, ssk] 3 times, k1, [k2tog, yo] 3 times, k3. Rep rows 1-4 for trellis pat.

SCARF (Make 2 pieces)

Cast on 154 sts. K 1 row. **Next 3 rows K2, *inc 1 st in next st, k5, sl 2, k1, p2sso, k5, inc 1 st in next st; rep from * to last 2 sts, k2. K 1 row.**

designed by margaret stove

(Continued on page 119)

fringed geometric wrap

intermediate

SIZES

One size fits all.

KNITTED MEASUREMENTS

Approx 24" x 72"/61cm x 183cm (not including fringe)

MATERIALS

• 2 2oz/57g skeins (each approx 118yd/108m) of La Lana Wools *Forever Random Fine* (wool ③) each in moonmist (A), emerald city (B), monet (C), yellow brick road (D), sweet lorraine (E), apassionada (F) and noche (G)

• 1 skein each in deep sea indigo glace (H), fairy queen (I), zulu prince (J) and rosemist (K)

• One pair size 10½ (6.5mm) needles OR SIZE TO OBTAIN GAUGE

• Size H/8 (5mm) crochet hook

GAUGES

• 14 sts and 32 rows = 4"/10 cm over garter st using size 10½ (6.5mm) needles.

• One square = 6"/15cm using size 10½ (6.5mm) needles.

TAKE TIME TO CHECK GAUGES.

Note: To change color when working in sc, draw new color through 2 lps on hook to complete sc.

SQUARE (make 48)

Refer to color placement diagram. With color 1, cast on 2 sts. **Next row** Knit. Cont in garter st, inc 1 st at beg of next 28 rows—30 sts. Cut yarn, leaving a 25"/63.5cm tail. Join color 2 with a knot leaving a 25"/63.5cm tail (tails are used for crochet embellishments). Cont in garter st, dec 1 st at beg of next 28 rows—2 sts. Cut yarn, draw through sts.

designed by valentina devine

(Continued on page 120)

summer lace shawl

expert

SIZES

To fit Small (Medium, Large). Directions are for smallest size with larger sizes in parentheses. If there is only one figure, it applies to all sizes.

KNITTED MEASUREMENTS

• 74½" x 23½"/189.5cm x 59.5cm at widest points (including edging)

MATERIALS

• 5 1¾oz/50g balls (each approx 119yd/110m) of GGH/Meunch Yarns *Mystik* (rayon ③) in #1 white

• Size 5 (3.75mm) circular needle, 29"/74cm long, OR SIZE TO OBTAIN GAUGE

• One double-pointed needle (dpn), any size under 5

GAUGE

18 sts and 32 rows = 4"/10cm over CHART I, using size 5 (3.75mm) needle.

TAKE TIME TO CHECK GAUGE.

CHART I (multiple of 6 sts, plus 1)

Rows 1 and 3 (WS) Purl. **Row 2** K1, *yo, ssk, k1, k2tog, yo, k1; rep from * to end. **Row 4** K1, *k1, yo, S2KP2, yo, k2; rep from * to end. Rep rows 1-4 for Chart I.

CHART II (begin on 19 sts)

Note: Sl sts purlwise wyif.

Row 1 (RS) Sl 1, k3, [yo, p2tog] twice, k4, yo, ssk, [yo, p2tog] twice, k1. **Row 2 (WS)** K1, [yo, p2tog] 3 times, k4, [yo, p2tog] twice, k4. **Row 3** Sl 1, k3, [yo, p2tog] twice, k3, k2tog, yo, k1, [yo, p2tog] twice, yo, [p1, k1] in last st. **Row 4** K1, yo, k2, [yo, p2tog] twice, k2, yo, p2tog, k2, [yo, p2tog] twice, k4. **Row 5** Sl 1, k3, [yo, p2tog] twice, k1, k2tog, yo, k3, [yo,

designed by maureen egan emlet

(Continued on page 121)

eyelet wrap

beginner

SIZES

One size fits all.

KNITTED MEASUREMENTS

Approx 14" x 83"/35.5cm x 211cm

MATERIALS

• 10 1¾oz/50g balls (each approx 65yd/60m) of Classic Elite Yarns *Sinful* (cashmere ⑤) in #20093 ecru

• One pair size 11 (8mm) needles OR SIZE TO OBTAIN GAUGE

GAUGE

13 sts and 14 rows = 4"/10cm over eyelet pat using size 11 (8mm) needles.

TAKE TIME TO CHECK GAUGE.

EYELET PATTERN (over an even number of sts)

Row 1 (RS) K2, *yo, k2tog; rep from * to last 2 sts, k2. **Row 2** K2, p to last 2 sts, k2. Rep rows 1 and 2 for eyelet pat.

WRAP

Cast on 46 sts. Work in eyelet pat for 83"/211cm, or desired length. Bind off.

FINISHING

Weave in ends. Block to measurements.

designed by rosemary drysdale

chevron stripe wrap

intermediate

SIZES

One size fits all.

KNITTED MEASUREMENTS

• Bust 72"/182.5cm

• Length from shoulder 32"/81.5cm (back) and 34"/86.5cm (fronts)

MATERIALS

• 4 3½oz/100g balls (each approx 98yd/90m) of Crystal Palace Yarns *Cotton Chenille* (cotton ⑤) each in #9598 black (A), #2801 mauve (B), #3387 med blue (C), #3441 forest green (D), #9717 navy (E), #4212 purple (F), #9121 burgundy (G), #5137 rust (H), #3433 brown (I), #1903 olive green (J)

• One pair size 8 (5mm) needles OR SIZE TO OBTAIN GAUGE

• Size 8 (5mm) circular needle 36"/90cm long

• St holder

GAUGE

16 sts and 24 rows = 4"/10cm over St st using size 8 (5mm) needles.

TAKE TIME TO CHECK GAUGE.

BACK

With A, cast on 144 sts. K 4 rows. Change to B and k 2 rows. Work in St st foll chart through row 186. This is end of back.

RIGHT FRONT

Row 187 (RS) Cont chart over first 72 sts for right front, place rem 72 sts on a holder for left front. Cont in right front sts only and cont chart pat through row 383. Change to B and p 2 rows. Change to A and p 3 rows. Bind off.

designed by kaffe fassett

(Continued on page 123)

winter shrug

very easy very vogue

SIZES

One size fits all.

KNITTED MEASUREMENTS

• Bust 42"/106cm

• Length (cuff to cuff) 60"/152cm

• Upper arm 22"/56cm

MATERIALS

• 9 .88oz/25g balls (each approx 92yd/84m) of GGH/Muench Yarns *Angora* (angora ④) in #40 black

• One pair each sizes 5 and 7 (3.75 and 4.5 mm) needles OR SIZE TO OBTAIN GAUGE

• Stitch markers

GAUGE

22 sts and 32 rows = 4"/10cm over k1, p2 rib (slightly stretched) using larger needles.

TAKE TIME TO CHECK GAUGE.

Note: Shrug is worked in one piece from cuff to cuff.

K1, P2 RIB (multiple of 3 sts plus 1)

Row 1 (RS) K1, *p2, k1; rep from * to end. **Row 2** K the knit sts and p the purl sts. Rep row 2 for k1, p2 rib.

BODY

With smaller needles, cast on 49 sts. Work in k1, p1 rib for 4"/10 cm, inc 4 sts evenly across last row—53 sts. Change to larger needles and cont as foll: **Next row (RS)** Work 5 sts in garter st, work k1, p2 rib over next 43 sts, work 5 sts in garter st. Cont as established, inc 1 st each side (inside of 5 sts garter st and into rib pat) alternately every 2nd and 4th row until there

designed by jean guirguis

(Continued on page 124)

wave-pattern wrap

very easy very vogue

SIZES

One size fits all.

KNITTED MEASUREMENTS

Approx 25" x 80"/63.5cm x 203cm

MATERIALS

• 1 3½oz/100g balls (each approx 55yd/50m) of Colinette Yarns/Unique Kolours *Point 5* (wool ⑤) each in ecru (A) and #144 cream tea (B)

• 1 3½oz/100g balls (each approx 189yd/175m) of Colinette Yarns/Unique Kolours *Mohair* (mohair/ wool/nylon ⑤) each in #63 mushroom (C), ecru (D) and soft sienna (E)

• 1 3½oz/100g balls (each approx 108yd/100m) of Colinette Yarns/Unique Kolours *Fandango* (cotton ⑤) in ecru (F)

• 1 3½oz/100g balls (each approx 184yd/170m) of Colinette Yarns/Unique Kolours *Wigwam* (cotton ⑤) in #144 cream tea (G)

• 1 3½oz/100g balls (each approx 108yd/100m) of Colinette Yarns/Unique Kolours *Isis* (viscose ⑤) in #144 cream tea (H)

• 1 3½oz/100g balls (each approx 101yd/94m) of Colinette Yarns/Unique Kolours *Zanziba* (viscose/nylon ⑤) each in #63 mushroom (I) and ecru (J)

• One pair size 19 (15mm) needles OR SIZE TO OBTAIN GAUGE

GAUGE

9 sts = 4"/10cm over wave pat using size 19 (15mm) needles.

TAKE TIME TO CHECK GAUGE.

designed by rebecca rosen

(Continued on page 124)

perfect ponchos

turtleneck capelet

very easy very vogue

SIZES

One size fits all.

KNITTED MEASUREMENTS

29"/73.5cm wide at lower edge by 16"/40cm deep to top of shoulder.

MATERIALS

• 6 1¾oz/50g balls (each approx 41yd/38m) of Berroco, Inc. *Chinchilla Bulky* (rayon ⑤) in #7525 brown (A)

• 8 .70oz/20g balls (each approx 63yd/58m) of Berroco, Inc. *Plume FX* (polyester ②) in #6743 brown (B)

• Size 11 (8mm) circular needles, one each 24"/60cm and 16"/40cm long OR SIZE TO OBTAIN GAUGE

• Stitch markers

GAUGE

9 sts and 11 rows = 4"/10cm over St st using 1 strand each A and B held tog and size 11 (8mm) needles.

TAKE TIME TO CHECK GAUGE.

Note: Work with 1 strand A and B held tog throughout.

CAPELET

Beg at lower edge with 1 strand A and B held tog and longer circular needle, cast on 130 sts. Join to work in rnds taking care not to twist sts in rnd. Place marker to mark beg of rnd. This is the center back. Working in St st, (knit every rnd), work even for 7 rnds or approx 2½"/6.5cm. **Dec rnd 1** K28, SKP, pm, k4, pm, k2tog, k57, SKP, pm, k4, k2tog, k29—126 sts. **Rnd 2** Knit. **Dec rnd 3** K to 2 sts before first marker, SKP, k4, k2tog, k to 2 sts before 2nd marker, SKP, k4, k2tog, k to end—122 sts. **Rnd 4** Knit. Rep rnds 3 and 4 14 times more—66 sts.

Note: Change to shorter circular needle when there are too few sts to fit needle.

designed by vladimir teriokhin

(Continued on page 125)

tweed poncho

very easy very vogue

SIZES

One size fits all.

KNITTED MEASUREMENTS

• Width at widest point 46"/117cm

• Length from center back neck (without fringe) 31"/78.5cm

MATERIALS

• 10 3½oz/100g balls (each approx 183yd/167m) of Tahki Yarns/Tahki•Stacy Charles, Inc. *Donegal Tweed* (wool ⑤) in #801 green

• Two size 13 (9mm) circular needles, 24"/60cm and 40"/100cm long

• Stitch markers

GAUGE

10 sts and 15 rows = 4"/10cm over St st using size 13 (9mm) needles and 2 strands of yarn held tog.

TAKE TIME TO CHECK GAUGE.

Notes: 1) Poncho is worked from the neck down. 2) Work with two strands of yarn held tog throughout.

PONCHO

With 2 strands of yarn held tog, cast on 56 sts. Join, taking care not to twist sts on needle. Place marker for end of rnd and sl marker every rnd. Work in k2, p2 rib for 9"/23cm. Note: When placing markers on the foll rnd, use different markers than the end of rnd marker for easier knitting. Slip all markers on every rnd.

Next rnd K1, pm (center back), k14, pm (center shoulder), k14, pm (center front), k14, pm (center shoulder), k13. **Next rnd** K1, yo, [k13, yo, k1, yo] 3 times, k13, yo. K 1 rnd. **Next rnd** K1, yo, k1 [k14, yo, k1, yo, k1] 3 times, k14, yo. K 1 rnd. **Next rnd** K1, yo, k2, [k15, yo, k1, yo, k2] 3 times, k15, yo. K 1 rnd.

designed by joan vass

(Continued on page 125)

cowl neck poncho

SIZES

To fit Small (Medium, Large). Directions are for smallest size with larger sizes in parentheses. If there is only one figure, it applies to all sizes.

KNITTED MEASUREMENTS

Width 40 (48, 54)"/101.5 (122, 137)cm

Length 28 (30, 32)"/71 (76, 81.5)cm

MATERIALS

• 30 (38, 44) 1¾oz/50g balls (each approx 102yd/94m) of Plymouth Yarns *Indiecita Alpaca Worsted Weight* (alpaca ③) in #401 grey

• Size 10½ (6.5mm) needles OR SIZE TO OBTAIN GAUGE

• Stitch holders

• Tapestry needle

• Small amount of polyester fiberfill

GAUGE

12 sts and 21 rows to 4"/10cm over Seed st, using size 10½ (6.5mm) needles and 2 strands of yarn held tog.

TAKE TIME TO CHECK GAUGE.

Note: Use 2 strands of yarn held tog throughout.

SEED STITCH

Row 1 (RS) *K1, p1; rep from *. **Row 2** K the purl sts and p the knit sts. Rep row 2 for seed st.

designed by nicky epstein

(Continued on page 126)

rectangular poncho

very easy very vogue

SIZES

One size fits all.

MATERIALS

• 7 1¾oz/50g hanks (each approx 75yd/69m) of Berroco, Inc. *Glacé* in #2437 yellow (rayon ④)

• One pair size 8 (5mm) needles OR SIZE TO OBTAIN GAUGE

• Two size 7 (4.5mm) dpn

GAUGE

18 sts and 24 rows = 4"/10cm over pat st using size 8 (5mm) needles.

TAKE TIME TO CHECK GAUGE

Note: Seam of poncho will hang asymmetrically.

PONCHO (make 2 pieces)

Cast on 60 sts. Working the first and last st of every row as a k1 for selvage st, work in St st until piece measures 28"/71cm. Bind off.

FINISHING

Sew cast-on edge of one piece to the first 13"/33cm of right lower side edge of 2nd piece. Sew bound-off edge of 2nd piece to the first 13"/33cm of right lower side edge of first piece.

I-cord trim/edging

Work I-cord trim around lower edge and neck of poncho as foll: With dpn cast on 3 sts. **Row 1** K2, k next st tog with 1 st from edge. Do not turn. Slide sts to beg of dpn and rep from * around for I-cord trim. Bind off. Work in same way around neck edge.

designed by victoria mayo

turtleneck poncho

intermediate

SIZES

One size fits all.

KNITTED MEASUREMENTS

• Approx 22"/56cm long (without fringe)

MATERIALS

• 20 1¾oz/50g balls (each approx 92yd/90m) of Jaeger Handknits *Natural Fleece* (wool ⑤) in #525 brown

• One pair size 13 (9mm) needles OR SIZE TO OBTAIN GAUGE

• Cable needle

• Stitch markers

GAUGE

11 sts and 15 rows = 4"/10cm over St st using size 13 (9mm) needles.

TAKE TIME TO CHECK GAUGE.

CABLE PATTERN (over 25 sts)

Row 1 (RS) [P1, k4] twice, [p1, k1] twice, p1, (k4, p1) twice. **Row 2** K1, p4, k1, p3, [k1, p1] 3 times, k1, p3, k1, p4, k1. **Row 3** P1, C4B, p1, k4, [p1, k1] twice, p1, k4, p1, C4F, p1. **Row 4** Rep row 2. **Row 5** P1, k4, p1, C6F, k1, C6B, p1, k4, p1. **Row 6** K1, p4, k1, p13, k1, p4, k1. **Row 7** P1, C4B, p1, k13, p1, C4F, p1. **Row 8** Rep row 6. **Row 9** P1, k4, p1, k13, p1, k4, p1. **Row 10** Rep row 6. **Row 11** Rep row 7. **Row 12** Rep row 6. **Row 13** P1, k4, p1, C6B, k1, C6F, p1, k4, p1. **Row 14** Rep row 2. **Row 15** Rep row 3. **Row 16** Rep row 4. Rep rows 1-16 for cable pat.

BACK

Cast on 137 sts. K 2 rows. Beg with a K row, work in St st for 1½"/4cm. **Next (dec) row (RS)** K29, k2tog tbl, pm, k1,

designed by martin storey

(Continued on page 127)

• Length 19"/48cm (before fringe)

• Width at lower edge approx 64"/162.5cm

MATERIALS

• 5 7½oz/250g skeins (each approx 310yd/286m) of Wool Pak Yarns NZ/Baabajoes Wool Company *14 Ply* (wool ⑤) in natural

• Scrap yarn

• One pair size 11 (8mm) needles OR SIZE TO OBTAIN GAUGE

• Cable needle

• Crochet hook size K/10½ (7mm)

• Tapestry needle

GAUGE

11 sts and 14 rows = 4"/10cm over chart pat using size 11 (8mm) needles and 2 strands held tog. To make swatch, cast on 20 sts and work first 20 sts of chart beg with row 9. The width should measure 5½"/14cm unsteamed.

Bobble

[K1, yo, k1] into st, turn, k on WS, turn, p on RS, turn k on WS, turn, k3tog.

Notes: **1** You may find it easier to use circular needle to accommodate the width of piece. **2** Scrap yarn cast on facilitates grafting of stitches at the side for a clean seam; however a regular cast on may be used. **3** All short row shaping is worked in space between cable pats. See stitch glossary page.

designed by teva durham

(Continued on page 128)

mock turtleneck poncho

very easy very vogue

SIZES

One size fits all.

KNITTED MEASUREMENTS

57" x 21½"/144.5cm x 54.5cm

MATERIALS

• 12 1¾oz/50g balls (each approx 108yd/ 97m) of Tahki Yarns/Tahki•Stacy Charles, Inc. *Dazzle* (wool ⑤) in #1459 orange/ brown multi

• Two size 10½ (6.5mm) circular needles, one 36"/90cm and one 16"/40cm long OR SIZE TO OBTAIN GAUGE

GAUGE

14 sts and 18 rows = 4"/10cm over St st using size 10½ (6.5mm) needles.

TAKE TIME TO CHECK GAUGE.

RIDGE PATTERN (in rows)

Row 1 (RS) Purl. **Row 2** Purl. **Row 3** Knit. **Row 4** Purl. Rep rows 1-4 for ridge pat in rows.

RIDGE PATTERN (in rounds)

Rnd 1 (RS) Purl. **Rnds 2-4** Knit. Rep rnds 1-4 for ridge pat in rnds.

BACK

With longer circular needle, cast on 200 sts. Work 4 row ridge pat (in rows) 6 times, work row 1.

Next row (WS) Cont ridge pat over first 20 sts, work in St st over center 160 sts, work in ridge pat to end. Cont in pats as established until piece measures 13"/33cm from beg.

designed by vladimir teriokhin

(Continued on page 130)

spiral lace capelet

intermediate

SIZES

One size fits all.

KNITTED MEASUREMENTS

Capelet

• Lower edge 45"/114cm

• Length 21"/53cm

Hat

• Circumference 18"/45.5cm

• Depth 12"/30.5cm

MATERIALS

• 6 1¾oz/50g balls (each approx 192yd/175m) of Filatura Di Crosa/Tahki•Stacy Charles, Inc. *Butterfly* (mohair/ acrylic ④) in #400 white

• Size 10½ (6.5mm) circular needle, 29"/74cm long OR SIZE TO OBTAIN GAUGE

• Size 10 (6mm) circular needle, 18"/45cm long

• One size 10 (6mm) dpn

• St marker

GAUGE

22 sts and 27 rnds = 6"/15cm over pat st using double strand of yarn and larger needles.

TAKE TIME TO CHECK GAUGE.

Note: Use a double strand of yarn throughout.

designed by lipp holmfeld

(Continued on page 131)

head into the cold

seed stitch cap

intermediate

SIZES

One size fits all.

KNITTED MEASUREMENTS

• Head circumference 22"/56cm

MATERIALS

• 2 3½oz/100g balls (each approx 60yd/50m) of Colinette/Unique Kolours *Point Five* (wool ®) in #122 hot pink (A)

• Small amount of a DK-weight wool in black (B)

• Size 10½ (6.5mm) circular needle, 16"/40cm long OR SIZE TO OBTAIN GAUGE

• 1 set (4) dpn size 10½ (6.5mm)

• Size F/5 (4mm) crochet hook

• Stitch markers

GAUGE

10 sts and 12 rows = 4"/10cm over seed st using size 10½ (6.5mm) needles.

TAKE TIME TO CHECK GAUGE.

SEED STITCH

Row 1 (RS) *K1, p1; rep from * to end. **Row 2** K the purl sts and p the knit sts. Rep row 2 for seed st.

HAT

With circular needle and A, cast on 52 sts. Pm and join, being careful not to twist sts. Work in seed st for 22 rnds. **Next (dec) rnd** *Work 11 sts seed st, k2tog; rep from * to end—48 sts. **Next (dec) rnd** *Work 6 sts seed st, k2tog; rep from * to end—42 sts. Change to dpn, place 14 sts on each needle. **Next rnd** *Work 6 sts seed st, k1; rep from * to end. **Next rnd**

designed by lipp holmfeld

(Continued on page 131)

diamond scarf

intermediate

SIZES

One size fits all.

KNITTED MEASUREMENTS

• Approx 7" x 50"/17.5 x 127cm

MATERIALS

• 3 1¾oz/50g balls (each approx 109yd/100m) of Noro/Knitting Fever, Inc., *Kureyon* (wool ④) in #40 blue/green multi

• One pair size 8 (5mm) needles OR SIZE TO OBTAIN GAUGE

• Bobbins

GAUGE

18 sts and 28 rows = 4"/10 cm over St st using size 8 (5mm) needles.

TAKE TIME TO CHECK GAUGE.

Notes: 1) To prepare bobbins for garter st blocks, work as foll: from first ball of yarn, cut a 200"/508cm length and wind onto bobbin for G1. Cont to cut 7 100"/254cm lengths and wind onto separate bobbins for colors G2, G3, G4, G5, G6, G7 and G8. Cont to wind more G1 to G8 bobbins from this ball as needed. 2) To prepare bobbins for St st blocks, work as foll: from second ball of yarn, cut 8 100"/254cm lengths and wind onto separate bobbins for colors S1, S2, S3, S4, S5, S6, S7 and S8. Cont to wind more S1 to S8 bobbins from this ball as needed. 3) When first and second balls are used up, wind third ball into two equal size balls. Use one ball to cut lengths for garter st blocks G1 to G8 and second ball to cut lengths for St st blocks S1 to S8.

SCARF

With G1, cast on 8 sts and work as foll: **Rows 1-9** Knit. **Row 10** With G1, k8, with G2, cast on 8 sts—16 sts. **Row 11 (RS)** With G2, k8, with S1, k8, with G3, cast on 8 sts—24 sts. **Rows 12, 14, 16** and **18** With G3, k8, with S1, p8, with G2, k8.

designed by jill gutman schoenfuss

(Continued on page 132)

garter-stitch flower scarf

very easy very vogue

KNITTED MEASUREMENTS

• 10" x 50"/25.5 x 127cm

MATERIALS

• 4 .87oz/25g balls (each approx 268yd/241m) of Filatura Di Crosa/Tahki•Stacy Charles, Inc. *Baby Kid Extra* (mohair/nylon ①) in #310 off white

• One pair size 10 (6mm) needles OR SIZE TO OBTAIN GAUGE

• Size US 7 (1.5mm) steel crochet hook

GAUGE

16 sts and 32 rows = 4"/10cm over garter st with 2 strands held together using size 10 (6mm) needles.

TAKE TIME TO CHECK GAUGE.

Note: Use 2 strands of yarn held tog throughout.

SCARF

With 2 strands held tog, cast on 40 sts. Work in garter st for 50"/127cm. Bind off.

CROCHETED FLOWERS (make 12)

With crochet hook ch 5, join with sl st to first ch to form ring. **Rnd 1** Ch 2 (counts as 1 sc), work 15 sc into ring, join with sl st to beg ch. **Rnd 2** [Ch 4, sk 2 sc, sl st in next sc] 5 times, end last rep sl st in base of beg ch. **Rnd 3** In each ch-4 sp around work (1 sc, 3 dc, 1 tr, 3 dc, 1sc), join with sl st to first sc. **Rnd 4** [Ch 5, sl st between next 2 sc (between petals)] 5 times, end sl st to base of beg ch. **Rnd 5** Ch 1, work (1 sc, 4 dc, 2 tr, 4 dc, 1 sc) in each ch-5 sp around, end sl st to beg ch. Sew 6 flowers evenly across each end of scarf.

lace-pattern scarf

intermediate

SIZES

One size fits all.

KNITTED MEASUREMENTS

Approx 8½" x 102"/21.5cm x 259cm

MATERIALS

• 4 3½oz/100g balls (each approx 165yd/158m) of Trendsetter Yarns *Dali* (cashmere ④) in #150 pink

• One pair each sizes 8 and 9 (5 and 5.5mm) needles OR SIZE TO OBTAIN GAUGE

GAUGE

16 sts and 20 rows = 4"/10cm over St st using larger needles.

TAKE TIME TO CHECK GAUGE.

SCARF

With smaller needles, cast on 49 sts.

Row 1 (RS) [K1, p1] twice, [k1tbl, p1] twice, [k1, p1] 17 times, [k1tbl, p1] twice, k1, p1, k1. **Row 2** [P1, k1] twice, [p1tbl, k1] twice, [p1, k1] 17 times, [p1tbl, k1] twice, p1, k1, p1. **Row 3** P1, k1, p2, [k1tbl, p1] twice, [k1, p1] 17 times, [k1tbl, p1] twice, p1, k1, p1. **Row 4** K1, p1, k2, [p1tbl, k1] twice, [p1, k1] 17 times, [p1tbl, k1] twice, k1, p1, k1. Rep rows 1 and 2 once more. Change to larger needles.

Beg chart

Beg with row 1, work 32 rows of chart until piece measures approx 100"/254cm from beg, end with row 1. Change to smaller needles and cont as foll:

Row 1 (RS) P1, k1, p2, [k1tbl, p1] twice, [k1, p1] 17 times, [k1tbl, p1] twice, p1, k1, p1. **Row 2** K1, p1, k2, [p1tbl, k1] twice, k2, p7, k2, [p1tbl, k1] twice, k4,[p1tbl, k1] twice, k1, p7, k3, [p1tbl, k1] twice, k1, p1, k1.

designed by anna mishka

(Continued on page 132)

multi-pink scarf

intermediate

SIZES

One size fits all.

KNITTED MEASUREMENTS

Approx 8" x 60"/20 x 151cm

MATERIALS

• 4 1¾oz/50g balls (each approx 109yd/100m) of Noro/Knitting Fever, Inc. *Kureyon* (wool ④) in #130 pink/purple multi

• One pair size 8 (5mm) needles OR SIZE TO OBTAIN GAUGE

• Bobbins

GAUGE

18 sts and 28 rows = 4"/10 cm over St st using size 8 (5mm) needles.

TAKE TIME TO CHECK GAUGE.

Notes: 1) For colors A and B, wind one ball into two equal size balls. 2) For colors C to J needed for charts 1 and 2, cut colors from another ball of yarn and wind each on a separate bobbin. The colors needed are: orange (C), burgundy D, periwinkle (E), magenta (F), pink (G), purple (H), plum (I) and grey/burgundy heather (J).

SEED STITCH

Row 1 (RS) *K1, p1; rep from * to end. **Row 2** Knit the p sts and purl the k sts. Rep row 2 for seed st.

SCARF

With A, cast on 32 sts. Work in seed st for 4 rows, end with a WS row.

Beg chart 1

Row 1 (RS) With A, work 4 sts in seed st, beg chart with st 1, work in St st to st 24, join B, work in seed st to end.

designed by jill gutman schoenfuss

(Continued on page 133)

ribbed hooded cowl

very easy very vogue

SIZES

One size fits all.

MATERIALS

Original Yarn

• 4 1¾oz/50g balls (each approx 126yd/115m) of Schoeller Wolle/Skacel Imports *Wollspass* (wool ②) in #6 fuchsia

Substitute Yarn

• 4 1¾oz/50g balls (each approx131yd/120m) of Jaeger HandKnits *Baby Merino* (wool ②) in #219 red

• One pair size 4 (3.5mm) knitting needles OR SIZE TO OBTAIN GAUGE

Note: The original yarn used for this hooded cowl is no longer available. A comparable substitute has been made, which is available at the time of printing. Check gauge of substitute yarns very carefully before beginning.

GAUGE

32 sts and 32 rows to 4"/10cm over k1, p1 rib using size 4 (3.5mm) needles.

TAKE TIME TO CHECK GAUGE.

HAT

Cast on 165 sts. **Row 1 (RS)** *K1, p1; rep from *, end k1. **Row 2** *P1, k1; rep from *, end p1. Rep last 2 rows until piece measures 17"/43cm. Bind off knitwise.

FINISHING

Sew side seam to form a tube.

designed by lipp holmfeld

(Continued on page 134)

leaf scarf

intermediate

SIZES

One size fits all.

KNITTED MEASUREMENTS

Approx 8" x 78"/20.5 x 198cm

MATERIALS

• 5 3½/100g balls (each approx 45yd/41m) of Blue Sky Alpaca *Bulky Alpaca* (alpaca/wool ⑤)

• One pair size 15 (10mm) needles OR SIZE TO OBTAIN GAUGE

GAUGE

8 sts and 12 rows = 4"/10cm over leaf st pat using size 15 (10mm) needles.

TAKE TIME TO CHECK GAUGE.

LEAF STITCH PATTERN

Row 1 and all WS rows Purl. **Row 2** P2, k9, yo, k1, yo, k3, SK2P, p2. **Row 4** P2, k10, yo, k1, yo, k2, SK2P, p2. **Row 6** P2, k3tog, k4, yo, k1, yo, k3 [yo, k1] twice, SK2P, p2. **Row 8** P2, k3tog, k3, yo, k1, yo, k9, p2. **Row 10** P2, k3tog, k2, yo, k1, yo, k10, p2. **Row 12** P2, k3tog, [k1, yo] twice, k3, yo, k1, yo, k4, SK2P, p2. Rep these 12 rows for leaf st pat.

SCARF

Cast on 20 sts. Work in leaf st pat until piece measures 78"/198cm. Bind off.

designed by veronica manno

ribbed draw-string hat

very easy very vogue

SIZES

One size fits all.

MATERIALS

Original Yarn

• 3 1¾oz/50g balls (each approx 140yd/128m) of Pingouin *4 Pingouins* (wool ②) in #69 lime green

Substitute Yarn

• 3 1¾oz/50g balls (each approx 176yd/162m) of Koigu Wool Designs *Premium Merino* (wool ②) in #2132 bright green

• One pair size 4 (3.5mm) knitting needles OR SIZE TO OBTAIN GAUGE

Note: The original yarn used for this hat is no longer available. A comparable substitute has been made, which is available at the time of printing. Check gauge of substitute yarns very carefully before beginning.

GAUGE

36 sts and 34 rows to 4"/10cm over k1, p1 rib (unstretched) using size 4 (3.5mm) needles.

TAKE TIME TO CHECK GAUGE.

HAT

Cast on 157 sts. **Row 1 (RS)** *K1, p1; rep from *, end k1. **Row 2** *P1, k1; rep from * end p1. Rep last 2 rows for 14"/35.5cm. **Next row (RS)** K1, *rib 3 sts, k2tog; rep from * end k1—126 sts. **Eyelet row** P1, *yo, rib 5 sts, yo, rib 3; rep from *, end rib 5. Rib 8 rows more or 156 sts. Bind off knitwise.

FINISHING

Sew side seam. Cut a strand 3yds/3m long and make a twisted cord. Thread cord through eyelet row and tie tightly. Make two pompoms and attach to end of cord.

designed by lipp holmfeld

aran scarf with knotted fringe

intermediate

SIZES

One size fits all.

KNITTED MEASUREMENTS

Approx 12" x 90"/30.5cm x 228.5cm

MATERIALS

• 17 1¾oz/50g balls (each approx 100yd/92m) of Plymouth Yarn *Indiecita Alpaca Worsted Weight* (alpaca ③) in #100 ecru

• One pair each sizes 8 and 10 (5 and 6mm) needles OR SIZE TO OBTAIN GAUGE

• Size H/8 (5mm) crochet hook

• Cable needle

GAUGE

17 sts and 14 rows = 4"/10cm over sand st using 2 strands of yarn and larger needles.

TAKE TIME TO CHECK GAUGE.

Note: Use 2 strands of yarn held tog throughout.

SAND STITCH

Row 1 (RS) *K1, p1; rep from * to end. **Row 2** Knit. Rep rows 1 and 2 for sand st.

6-ST RIGHT CABLE PATTERN (over 6 sts)

Rows 1, 3 and 7 (RS) Knit. **Rows 2, 4, 6 and 8** Purl. **Row 5** Sl 3 sts to cn and hold to back, k3, k3 from cn. Rep rows 1-8 for 6-st right cable pat.

6-ST LEFT CABLE PATTERN (over 6 sts)

designed by lisa buccellato

(Continued on page 134)

cabled helmut hat

intermediate

SIZES

One size fits all.

KNITTED MEASUREMENTS

• Circumference approx 21"/53cm

• Depth 8½"/21.5cm

MATERIALS

• 3 1¾oz/50g hanks (each approx 109yd/100m) of Cherry Tree Hill *Possum Paints Worsted* (merino/possum ④) in birches

• One set (4) size 11 (8mm) dpn OR SIZE TO OBTAIN GAUGE

• Size 11 (8mm) circular needle, 16"/40cm long

• Cable needle (cn)

• St marker

GAUGE

12 sts and 16 rows = 4"/10cm over St st using 2 strands of yarn and size 11 (8mm) needles.

TAKE TIME TO CHECK GAUGE.

Note: Work with 2 strands of yarn held tog throughout.

EARFLAPS (make 2)

Using 2 dpn and 2 strands of yarn, cast on 5 sts. Working back and forth in rows, k2 rows. **Inc row 1 (WS)** K2, yo, p1, yo, k2. **Next row (RS)** Knit. **Inc row 2 (WS)** K2, yo, purl to last 2 sts, yo, k2. **Next row** Knit. Rep last 2 rows 3 times more—15 sts. Keeping 2 k sts at each end, work even for 5 rows more. (The last row is a WS row). Leave sts on hold and cut yarn for first earflap leaving a long end. For 2nd earflap, do not cut yarn and beg base of hat.

designed by mari lynn patrick

(Continued on page 135)

geometric scarf

intermediate

SIZES

One size fits all.

KNITTED MEASUREMENTS

Approx 5½ x 63½"/14 x 161cm

MATERIALS

• 2 1¾/50g balls (each approx 175yd/161m) of Koigu Wool Design *Premium Merino* (wool ②) in #2400 black (MC)

• 1 ball each in # 1500 turquoise (A), #2340S olive (B), #1230 gold (C) and #2151 aqua (D)

• One set size 4 (3.5mm) dpn OR SIZE TO OBTAIN GAUGE

• Size 4 (3.5mm) circular needle, 29"/74cm long

GAUGE

23 sts and 46 rows = 4"/10cm over garter st using size 4 (3.5mm) dpn.

TAKE TIME TO CHECK GAUGE.

GRANNY SQUARE PATTERN (worked in garter st over 124 sts)

Cast on 124 sts and divide evenly over 4 needles. Join to form square by slipping first cast on st from RH needle to LH needle.

Rnd 1 S2KP, k to last st on first needle, sl last st to second needle, S2KP, k to last st on second needle, sl last st to third needle, S2KP, k to last st on third needle, sl last st to fourth needle, S2KP, k to end. **Rnd 2** *Sl first st with yarn in back, p to end of needle; rep from * to last st on needle 4, sl last st to needle 1. Rep these 2 rnds 13 times more.

Final rnd *S2KP, sl last st on first needle to second needle; rep from * around until 1 st remains on each needle. Cut yarn and thread through rem sts. Fasten tightly. 29 rnds for granny square pat.

Notes: 1) Cast on with MC for all squares. 2) Use MC for final rnd for all squares.

designed by barbara venishnick

(Continued on page 136)

seed stitch hat
and scarf

very easy very vogue

SIZES

One size fits all.

KNITTED MEASUREMENTS

• Hat circumference 19½"/49.5cm

• Scarf width 8"/20.5cm

• Scarf length 66"/167.5cm

MATERIALS

Hat

• 2 3½oz/100g balls (each approx 66yd/61m) of Reynolds/JCA *Blizzard* (alpaca/acrylic ⑤) in #673 tan

Scarf

• 5 balls

• One pair size 10½ (6.5mm) needles OR SIZE TO OBTAIN GAUGE

GAUGE

10½ sts and 18 rows = 4"/10 cm over seed st using size 10½ (6.5mm) needles.

TAKE TIME TO CHECK GAUGE.

SEED STITCH

Row 1 K1, *p1, k1; rep from * to end. **Row 2** Knit the p sts and purl the k sts. Rep row 2 for seed st.

HAT

Cast on 19 sts.

designed by gayle bunn

(Continued on page 136)

tea cozy hat

intermediate

SIZES

One size fits all.

MATERIALS

• 2 3½oz/100g balls (each approx 127yds/117m) of Classic Elite Yarns *Montera* (wool ④) in #3827 wine (MC).

• 1 ball in #11 cream tweed (CC)

• One pair each sizes 6 and 9 (4 and 5.5mm) needles OR SIZE TO OBTAIN GAUGE

• Stitch markers

GAUGE

16 sts and 19 rows = 4"/10cm over chart 1 using size 9 (5.5mm) needles.

TAKE TIME TO CHECK GAUGE.

Note: 1) Two selvage sts are included and are not reflected in finished measurements. 2) When changing colors, twist yarns on WS to prevent holes. 3) Work all charts in St st.

HAT

With smaller needles, cast on *1 st with MC, 1 st with CC; rep from * 39 times more, end cast on 1 st with MC — 81 sts. With MC, k 2 rows. **Next row** P1CC, *p7MC, p1CC; rep from *. **Next row** K2CC, *k5MC, k3CC; rep from *, end last rep k2CC. With MC, p 1 row, then k 1 row. **Next row** P1CC, *p1MC, p1CC; rep from *. With MC, p 2 rows (turning ridge), then beg with k row and work 4 rows in St st. **Next row (WS)** With MC, purl, inc 11 sts evenly across — 92 sts. Change to larger needles and beg with a k row, work 10 rows in St st.

Row 1 Beg as indicated, work to rep, work 8-st rep 11 times, end as indicated. Work through chart row 18. With MC, k 1 row, then p 1 row.

designed by gayle bunn

(Continued on page 137)

outerwear set

intermediate

SIZES

One size fits all.

KNITTED MEASUREMENTS

• Head circumference 19½"/49.5cm

• Scarf 7½" x 72"/19 x 183cm

• Fingerless mitten length 16½"/42cm

MATERIALS

• 4 4oz/113g balls (each approx 125yd/114m) of Brown Sheep Yarn Co. *Lambs Pride Bulky* (wool ⑤) in #03 grey heather (MC)

• 1 ball each in M18 aztec turquoise (A), #110 orange you glad (B), #23 fuchsia (C), #155 lemon drop (D), #59 periwinkle (E) and #120 limeade (F)

• One pair each sizes 8 and 10½ (5 and 6.5mm) needles OR SIZE TO OBTAIN GAUGES

• One spare size 10½ (6.5mm) needle or dpn

• Two ½"/13mm buttons (for fingerless mittens)

GAUGES

12 sts and 18 rows = 4"/10 cm over St st using larger needles.

11 sts and 24 rows = 4"/10 cm over garter st using larger needles.

TAKE TIME TO CHECK GAUGES.

Note: Scarf is worked on the diagonal.

designed by alida porter

(Continued on page 138)

pompom hat

intermediate

SIZES

One size fits all.

KNITTED MEASUREMENTS

• Head circumferance 20"/51cm

MATERIALS

• 2 3½oz/100g balls (each approx 215yd/196m) of Colorado Yarns *Knitaly* (wool ④) in #3266 rose

• One each sizes 5 and 6 (3.75 and 4mm) circular knitting needles 16"/40cm OR SIZE TO OBTAIN GAUGE

• 1 set (4) size 6 (4mm) double-pointed needles (dpn)

• Stitch marker

GAUGE

20 sts and 32 rows = 4"/10cm over double seed st using size 6 (4mm) needles.

TAKE TIME TO CHECK GAUGE.

Note: Change to dpn when there are too few sts to fit around circular needle.

DOUBLE SEED STITCH

Rnds 1 and 2 *K1, p1; rep from * around. **Rnds 3 and 4** *p1, k1; rep from * around. Rep rnds 1-4 for double seed st.

HAT

With smaller needle, cast on 100 sts. Join, taking care not to twist sts. Place marker for end of rnd. P 5 rnds. K 1 rnd. Change to larger needle. Work in double seed st for 3"/7.5cm. K 1 rnd. P 3 rnds. **Next rnd** *K3, k2tog; rep from * around—80 sts. Work in double seed st for 7 rnds. **Next rnd** *K3, k2tog; rep from * around—64 sts. P 3 rnds. **Next rnd** *K3, k2tog; rep from *, end k4—52 sts. Work in double seed st for 5 rnds. **Next rnd** *K1, k2tog; rep from *, end k1—35 sts. P 3 rnds.

designed by carol spier for lola millinery

(Continued on page 140)

sherpa hat and scarf

very easy very vogue

SIZES

One size fits all.

KNITTED MEASUREMENTS

Hat

• Head circumference 18"/45.5cm

Scarf

• 5½"/14cm x 37"/94cm (at longest point)

MATERIALS

Hat

• 3 1¾oz/50g balls (each approx 88yd/80m) of Filatura Di Crosa/Tahki•Stacy Charles, Inc. *Luna* (wool ④) in #204 ecru

Scarf

• 4 balls in #204 ecru

• One pair each sizes 10 and 10½ (6 and 6.5mm) needles OR SIZE TO OBTAIN GAUGE

• One set (4) dpn size 10 (6mm)

GAUGE

14 sts and 28 rows = 4"/10cm over garter st using larger needles.

TAKE TIME TO CHECK GAUGE.

TWISTED RIB

Row 1 *K1 tbl, p1; rep from * to end. **Row 2** K the knit sts tbl, p the purl sts. Rep row 2 for twisted rib.

designed by lipp holmfeld

(Continued on page 141)

cable scarf

intermediate

SIZES

One size fits all.

KNITTED MEASUREMENTS

Approx 9½" x 66"/24 x 167.5cm (not including fringe)

MATERIALS

• 4 3½oz/100g balls (each approx 78yd/71m) of Patons *UpCountry* (wool ⑤) in #80914 oak (A)

• 4 balls in #80906 soft cream (B)

• One pair size 11 (8mm) needles OR SIZE TO OBTAIN GAUGE

• Cable needle

• Size J/10 (6mm) crochet hook

GAUGE

11 sts and 16 rows = 4"/10 cm over St st using size 11 (8mm) needles.

TAKE TIME TO CHECK GAUGE.

SCARF

Note: When casting on each color, leave a 10"/25.5cm tail for fringe. Cast on as foll: [with A, cast on 2 sts, with B, cast on 2 sts] 8 times—32 sts.

Beg cable pat

Rows 1 and 3 (RS) [With B, k2, with A, k2] 8 times. **Row 2 and all WS rows** [With A, p2, with B, p2] 8 times. **Row 5** With B, k2, 8-st RC, with A, k2, 8-st LC, with B, k2, 8-st RC, with A, k2. **Rows 7 and 9** Rep row 1. **Row 10** Rep row 2. Rep rows 1-10 for cable pat until piece measures 66"/167.5cm from beg, end with row 8. Bind off each color leaving 10"/25.5cm tails.

designed by gayle bunn

(Continued on page 141)

snowflake hat

experienced

SIZES

One size fits all.

MATERIALS

• 2 1¾oz/50g balls (each approx 102 yds/94m) of Plymouth Yarns *Indiecita Alpaca Worsted* (alpaca ③) in #201 cream (MC), #208 taupe (A), #2020 burgundy (B) and #206 dark camel (C)

• Size 5 (3.75mm) double pointed needles (dpn), OR SIZE TO OBTAIN GAUGE

• Size 5 (3.75mm) circular needle, 16"/40cm

• Size D/3 (3mm) crochet hook

• Cable needle (cn)

• St markers

GAUGE

24 sts and 30 rows = 4"/10cm over St st using size 6 (4mm) needles.

TAKE TIME TO CHECK GAUGE.

Note: 1) Change to dpn when necessary. 2) Work chart in rnds by reading every row from right to left.

GARTER CHECK PAT (over 14 sts)

Row 1 (RS) K3A, *k2B, k2A; rep from *, end K2B, k3A. **Row 2** K3A, *k2B, p2A; rep from *, end k2B, k3A. **Row 3** K3A; *k2A, k2MC; rep from *, end k5A. **Row 4** K3A, *p2A, k2MC; rep from *, end p2A, k3A. Rep rows 1-4 for garter check pat.

HAT

With circular needle and A, cast on 112 sts. Being careful not to twist sts, place marker (pm) and join. Work in circular garter st (k1 rnd, p1 rnd) as foll: 4 rnds with A, 2 rnds with B, end at joining marker. Place separate marker on first rnd

designed by michele rose

(Continued on page 142)

basic scarf

very easy very vogue

SIZE

One size fits all.

KNITTED MEASUREMENTS

• Approx 8" x 54"/20.5 x 137cm

MATERIALS

• 2 5¼oz/150g ball (each approx 100yd/92m) of Mango Moon *Recycled Silk* (silk ⑤) in multi (A)

• 1 3¾oz/120g ball (each approx 350yd/323m) of Mango Moon *Mohair* (kid mohair/nylon ④) in pink (B)

• One pair size 10 (6mm) needles OR SIZE TO OBTAIN GAUGE

GAUGE

13 sts and 20 rows = 4"/10cm in St st using size 10 (6mm) needles and 1 strand each A and B held tog.

TAKE TIME TO CHECK GAUGE.

Note: Use 1 strand each A and B held tog throughout.

SCARF

With 1 strand each A and B held tog, cast on 24 sts and work in garter st for 6 rows. Keeping first and last 4 sts in garter st, work center 16 sts in St st until piece measures 21"/53.5cm from beg. Work in k2, p2 rib over all sts for 12"/30.5cm. Keeping first and last 4 sts in garter st, work center 16 sts in St st until piece measures 52½"/133.5cm from beg. Work 6 rows in garter sts. Bind off all sts.

designed by veronica manno

• 8" x 66"/20.5 167.5cm

MATERIALS

Hat

• 2 3½oz/100g balls (each approx 78yd/71m) of Patons *Up Country* (wool ⑤) in #80914 oak (MC)

• 1 ball each in #80913 deep oak (A) and #80906 soft cream (B)

Scarf

• 3 balls in #80914 oak (MC) and

• 1 ball each in #80913 deep oak (A) and #80906 soft cream (B)

• One pair size 10½ (6.5mm) needles OR SIZE TO OBTAIN GAUGE

GAUGE

13 sts and 18 rows = 4"/10 cm over St st using size 10½ (6.5mm) needles.

TAKE TIME TO CHECK GAUGE.

HAT

With MC, cast on 62 sts. Work in k2, p2 rib for 4½"/11.5cm, dec 1 st in center of last WS row—61 sts. Work in St st for 2 rows.

designed by gayle bunn

head into the cold

(Continued on page 143)

fair isle hat

intermediate

SIZES

One size fits all.

KNITTED MEASUREMENTS

• Circumference approx 21"/53cm

MATERIALS

• 1 1¾oz/50g ball (each approx 114yd/105m) of Koigu Wool Designs *Kersti Merino Crepe* (wool ④) each in #1014 blue (A), #1520 lime (B), #1515 aqua (C), #1100 red (D), #1150 pink (E) and #1190 orange (F).

• One size 6 (4mm) circular needle, 16"/40cm long

• One set (4) dpn size 6 (4mm)

• Size E/4 (3.5mm) crochet hook

• St markers

GAUGE

21 sts and 32 rows = 4"/10 cm in St st over charts using size 6 (4mm) circular needle.

TAKE TIME TO CHECK GAUGE.

HAT

With A and circular needle, cast on 112 sts. Join, taking care not to twist sts on needle. Place marker for end of end and sl marker every rnd. K 3 rnds. **Next 2 rnds** *K1 A, k1 B; rep from * around. With A, k 2 rnds. **Next rnd** *K1 E, k1 A; rep from * around. With D, k 1 rnd. With B, k 1 rnd. With A, k 2 rnds. With C, k 1 rnd. Work 11 rnds of chart 1 (working 14-st rep 8 times). With A, k 2 rnds. With B, k 1 rnd. With D, k 1 rnd. With C, k 1 rnd. **Next (dec) rnd** With C, k6, *k2tog, k12; rep from *, end last rep k6—104 sts. **Next rnd** K1 F, *k5 A, k3 F; rep from *, end k2 F. With C, k 1 rnd. Work 5 rnds of chart 2 (working 8-st rep 13 times). With A, k 1 rnd. **Next (dec) rnd** *K1 A, k1 E; rep from *, AT SAME TIME work

designed by pam allen

(Continued on page 144)

beaded scarf

experienced

SIZES

One size fits all.

KNITTED MEASUREMENTS

• Approx 8¼" x 39"/21 x 99cm

MATERIALS

• 4 .88oz/25g balls (each approx 145yd/130m) of Knit One Crochet Too *Richesse et Soie* (cashmere/silk ②) in #9510 taupe

• One pair size 3 (3.25mm) needles OR SIZE TO OBTAIN GAUGE

• Two size 10 or 12 beading needles

• Two ½oz tubes Japanese seed beads, shiny black

• One ½oz tube Japanese seed beads, matte black

• 600 4mm glass abacus beads, black

• 60 6x4mm glass teardrop beads, black

• 200 4mm glass fire polished beads, black

• Nymo black beading thread, size B

• Bead wax

GAUGE

29 sts and 24 rows = 4"/10cm over pat st using size 3 (3.25mm) needles.

TAKE TIME TO CHECK GAUGE.

SEED STITCH

Row 1 (RS) *K1, p1; rep from * to end. **Row 2** K the purl sts and p the knit sts. Rep row 2 for seed st.

designed by laura glazier

(Continued on page 145)

his-and-hers

ribbed hat and scarf set

very easy very vogue

SIZES

One size fits all.

KNITTED MEASUREMENTS

• Hat circumference 18½"/47cm

• Scarf width 6"/15.5cm

• Scarf length 51"/129.5cm

MATERIALS

Hat

• 1 3½oz/100g hanks (each approx 125yd/115m) of Colinette Yarns/Unique Kolours *Prism* (wool/cotton ⑤) in #76 lichen

Scarf

• 2 hanks in #76 lichen

• One pair size 9 (5.5mm) needles OR SIZE TO OBTAIN GAUGE

GAUGE

15 sts and 20 rows = 4"/10cm over k3, p2 rib (slightly stretched) using size 9 (5.5mm) needles.

TAKE TIME TO CHECK GAUGE.

Note: Hat can also be worked in the round on double pointed needles with no seaming.

K3, P2 RIB (multiple of 5 sts)

Row 1 (RS) *K3, p2; rep from * to end. **Row 2** K the knit sts and p the purl sts. Rep row 2 for k3, p2 rib.

HAT

Cast on 70 sts. Work in k3, p2 rib for 7½"/19cm.

designed by veronica manno

(Continued on page 146)

Scarf

• 10½"/26.5cm wide x 63"/160cm long (before sewing to scarf)

• 9½"/24cm wide x 60"/152cm long (after sewing to scarf)

Socks

• Leg width 8½"/21.5cm

• Foot length 10½"/26.5cm

MATERIALS

Scarf

• 5 1¾oz/50g balls (each approx 181yds/167m) of Lana Gatto/Needful Yarns *Wool Gatto* (wool ③) in #5000 black (A)

• 1 ball each in #8000 white (B) and #2536 turquoise (C)

• One pair size 4 (3.5mm) needles OR SIZE TO OBTAIN GAUGE

• Bobbins

• One purchased black fabric scarf with fringe 9½" x 60"/24 x 152cm

Socks

• 2 11¾oz/50g balls (each approx 181yds/167m) of Lana Gatto/Needful Yarns and Things *Wool Gatto* (wool ③) in #5000 black (A)

• 1 ball each in #8000 white (B) and #2536 turquoise (C)

• One set (5) size 3 (3mm) double pointed needles (dpn)

folk hat

experienced

SIZES

One size fits all.

KNITTED MEASUREMENTS

• Head circumference 21"/53.5cm

MATERIALS

• 2 1¾oz/50g balls (each approx 105yd/96m) of Indiecita/Plymouth Yarns *3 ply Sport Weight Alpaca* (alpaca ②) each in #500 black (A), #100 cream (B), #195 brown (C) and #207 sand (D)

(Continued on page 149)

andes cap and scarf

experienced

SIZES

One size fits all.

KNITTED MEASUREMENTS

• Head circumference 20"/50.5cm

MATERIALS

3 1¾oz/50g balls (each approx 109yd/100m) of Classic Elite Yarns *Inca Alpaca* (alpaca ②) each in #1197 lt green (A); 1 ball each in #1155 copper tweed (B); #1158 red (C); #1127 purple (D); #1135 lt olive green (E); #1136 caramel (F); #1124 blue (G); #1117 yellow (H); #1132 rose (I) and #1142 plum (J)

(Continued on page 150)

both designed by pam allen

cabled tri-color scarf

intermediate

KNITTED MEASUREMENTS

• 7 x 55"/17.5 x 139.5cm

MATERIALS

• 2 4oz/125g balls (each approx 130yd/120m) of Fiesta Yarns *Kokopelli* (mohair/wool ④) in #K01 black (A)

• 1 ball each in #K13 brown (B) and #K07 camel (C)

• One pair size 8 (5mm) needles, OR SIZE TO OBTAIN GAUGE

• Cable needle

GAUGE

18 sts and 22 rows= 4"/10cm over cable pat using size 8 (5mm) needles.

TAKE TIME TO CHECK GAUGE.

CABLE PATTERN (multiple of 8 sts plus 1)

Row 1 (RS) P1, *k7, p1; rep from * to end. **Row 2** K1, *p7, k1; rep from * to end. **Row 3** Rep row 1. **Row 4** Rep row 2. **Row 5** P1, *sl 4 sts to cn and hold to back, k3, k4 from cn, p1; rep from * to end. **Row 6** Rep row 2. Rep rows 1-6 for cable pat.

SCARF

With A, cast on 49 sts. *With A, work in cable pat for 18 rows. Change to B, cont in cable pat for 18 rows. Change to A, cont in cable pat for 18 rows. Change to C, cont in cable pat for 18 rows; rep from * 3 times more. With A, work in cable pat for 18 rows. Bind off.

FINISHING

Block lightly. Weave in ends.

designed by jean guirguis

nordic set

intermediate

SIZES

One size fits all.

KNITTED MEASUREMENTS

Scarf

• 13"/33cm wide x 68"/173cm long (folded in half lengthwise)

Hat

• Head circumference 21½"/54.5cm

MATERIALS

• 5 4oz/125g skeins (each approx 200yd/184m) of Cherry Tree Hill Yarns *Fusion* (mohair/rayon ④) in black (A)

• 3 skeins in turquoise (B)

• One pair size 6 (4mm) needles OR SIZE TO OBTAIN GAUGE

GAUGE

18 sts and 18 rows = 4"/10cm over St st foll chart using size 6 (4mm) needles.

TAKE TIME TO CHECK GAUGE.

Notes: 1) Scarf is worked in one straight piece that is folded in half lengthwise and sewn tog at lower and side edges.

2) Stitch multiples for each pattern segment are indicated by boxes around the sts.

SCARF

Beg at one lower end, with A cast on 120 sts. K 1 row, p 1 row.

Beg chart 1

Row 1 (RS) Work 8-st rep of pat 15 times. Cont to foll chart, adjusting st reps as necessary, for each pattern segment through row 153 of chart. Then beg at row 141, turn chart upside down and foll chart 1 backwards to row 1. Work 2 rows

designed by vladimir teriokhin

(Continued on page 153)

argyle ties

experienced

MATERIALS

• 1 1¾oz/50g balls (each approx 225yd/210m) of Schoeller Stahl/Skacel Collection *Fortissimia Socka* (wool ①) in #5 charcoal (MC)

• 1 ball #10575 charcoal; #1035 jeans; #1005 red; #1089 variegated green; #1072 cream

• One pair size 2 (2.75mm) needles OR SIZE TO OBTAIN GAUGE

• Bobbins

GAUGE

• 32 sts and 40 rows = 4"/10cm over St st using size 2 (2.75mm) needles.

TAKE TIME TO CHECK GAUGE.

Notes: 1) Use a separate bobbin for each diamond. 2) When changing colors, twist yarns on WS to avoid holes.

LARGE POINT

With MC, using open cast on method, cast on 59 sts. Work in St st for 2 rows. **Next row (RS)** Cut yarn, sl 29 sts to RH needle, rejoin yarn, k1, sl 1 turn. **Next row (WS)** P3, sl 1, turn. **Next row** K5, sl 1, turn. **Next row** P7, sl 1, turn. **Next row** K9, sl 1, turn. **Next row** P11, sl 1, turn. **Next row** K13, sl 1, turn. **Next row** Purl across as foll: 1 MC, 1 CC, 11 MC, 1 CC, 1 MC, sl 1 turn. **Next row** Knit across as foll: with new ball, 1 MC, 3 CC, 9 MC, 3 CC, with new ball 1 MC, sl 1, turn. Cont in this way to work 2 more sts every row and foll chart for color pat, until all sts are worked. Cont to sl the first st of every row and work these edge sts in MC for selvage. Dec 1 st each side every 10th row until there are 23 sts and piece measures 19"/48cm from the point. Work even until piece measures 46"/117cm from point. Inc 1 st each side every 10th row until there are 41 sts, end with a WS row.

SMALL POINT

Next row (RS) Work in pat to last 2 sts, wyib, sl next st, bring yarn to front of work between needles, sl same st back to LH needle (1 knit st wrapped). Turn. **Next row (WS)** Work to last 2 sts, wyif, sl next st, bring yarn to back between needles, sl

(Continued on page 154)

MATERIALS

• 2 2oz/70g balls (each approx 80yd/72m) of La Lana Wool *Blanca Handspun* (wool ④) in white

• One pair size 7 (4.5mm) needles OR SIZE TO OBTAIN GAUGE

• Two size 6 (4mm) dpn

• ¼yd/.25m white silk or linen for lining (optional)

GAUGE

18 sts = 4"/10cm over diagonal st using size 7 (4.5mm) needles.

TAKE TIME TO CHECK GAUGE.

DIAGONAL STITCH (multiple of 4 sts)

Row 1 (RS) *P2, k2; rep from * to end. **Row 2** *K1, p2, k1; rep from * to end. **Row 3** *K2, p2; rep from * to end. **Row 4** *P1, k2, p1; rep from * to end. Rep rows 1 to 4 for diagonal st.

BAG

With larger needles, cast on 36 sts for first half. Work in diagonal st for 7½"/19cm, end with a WS row. K 5 rows for top. Bind off knitwise. With WS facing and larger needles, pick up 36 stitches along bottom edge of purse. Work 2nd half as for first half.

men's
cabled mittens

intermediate

SIZE

One size.

MATERIALS

• 2 1¾oz/50g balls (each approx 153yd/140m) of Filatura Di Crosa/Tahki•Stacy Charles, Inc. *Cashmere* (cashmere ④) in #208 tan

• One set (4) size 3 (3.25mm) double pointed needles (dpn) OR SIZE TO OBTAIN GAUGE

• Cable needle (cn)

(Continued on page 155)

designed by jacquelyn smyth

women's
cabled gloves

intermediate

SIZE

One size.

MATERIALS

• 1 1¾oz/50g hank (each approx 319yd/ 295m) of Jilly Knitwear *100% Cashmere* (cashmere ①) in cardinal

• One pair each sizes 00 and 2 (2 and 2.75mm) needles OR SIZE TO OBTAIN GAUGE

• Cable needle (cn)

(Continued on page 156)

designed by jilly parker

basic cable sock

intermediate

SIZES

One size fits all.

MATERIALS

• 3 1 ¾oz/50g balls (each approx 129yd/118m) of Wendy's *Merino DK* (wool ③) in #329 ecru

• One set (4) size 4 (3.5mm) double-pointed knitting needles OR SIZE TO OBTAIN GAUGE.

• Cable needle (cn)

GAUGE

32 sts and 40 rnds to 4"/10cm over cable pat.

TAKE TIME TO CHECK GAUGE.

Cable Pattern

Rnds 1, 2 and 4 *K4, p1, k2, p1; rep from * around. **Rnd 3** *Sl 2 sts to cn and hold to back, k2, k2 from cn, p1, k2, p1; rep from * around. Rep rnds 1-4 for cable pat.

SOCK

Cast on 52 sts. Divide sts evenly onto 3 needles. Join, taking care not to twist sts. Work in k2, p2 rib for 2"/5cm, inc 12 sts evenly on last rnd—64 sts. Work in cable pat until sock measures 8"/20.5cm.

Divide for heel

Next rnd Work first 16 sts, place next 32 sts on 2 needles for the instep. Slide the last 16 sts onto the first needle for a total of 32 heel sts.

Heel flap

Work back and forth on heel sts as foll: **Row 1 (WS)** Sl first stitch, p to end. Row 2 *Slip 1 purlwise wyib, k1; rep from

designed by Theresa Gaffey

(Continued on page 157)

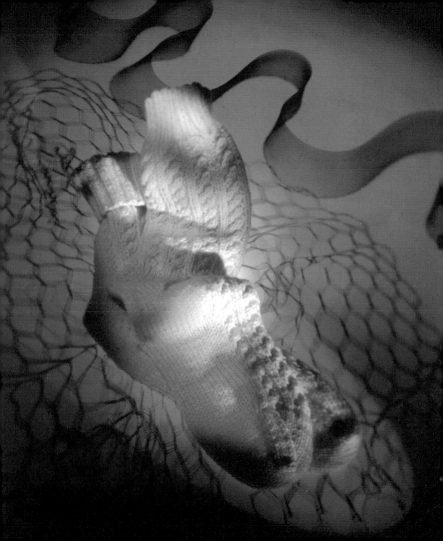

golf club covers

argyle

intermediate

SIZES

One size only.

MATERIALS

(for two covers)

• 1 3½oz/100g ball (each approx 185yd/ 170m) of Reynolds/JCA *Saucy* (cotton ③) each in #800 white (MC), #265 navy (A), #361 red (B) and #536 green (C)

• One pair size 4 (3.5mm) needles OR SIZE TO OBTAIN GAUGE

(Continued on page 158)

gingham

very easy very vogue

SIZES

One size only.

MATERIALS

• 1 1¾oz/50g ball (each approx 108yd/100m) of Tahki Yarns/Tahki•Stacy Charles, Inc. *Cotton Classic* (cotton ③) each in #3841 lt blue (MC), #3882 med blue (A), #3001 white (B) and #3856 navy (C)

• One pair size 4 (3.5mm) needles OR SIZE TO OBTAIN GAUGE

GAUGE

26 sts and 54 rows = 4"/10cm over check pat using size 4 (3.5mm) needles.

TAKE TIME TO CHECK GAUGE.

CHECK PATTERN (multiple of 4 sts plus 2)

Row 1 (WS) With A, purl. **Row 2** With B, k1, sl 1 wyib, *k2, sl 2 wyib; rep from *, end k2, sl 1 wyib, k1. **Row 3** With B,

(Continued on page 159)

designed by jacquelyn smith

stitch glossary

P2tog tbl P 2 sts tog through the back loops.

Ssk Sl 2 sts knitwise, one at a time, to RH needle, then insert LH needle into fronts of these 2 sts and k them tog.

S2KP Sl 2, k1, pass 2 sl sts over.

S2KP2 Sl 2 sts tog knitwise, k1, p2sso.

24-st LC Sl 12 sts to cn and hold to front, [k2, p2] 3 times, work sts from cn as foll: [k2, p2] 3 times.

24-st RC Sl 12 sts to cn and hold to back, [k2, p2] 3 times, work sts from cn as foll: [k2, p2] 3 times.

C4B Sl 2 sts to cn and hold to back, k2, k2 from cn.

C4F Sl 2 sts to cn and hold to front, k2, k2 from cn.

C6B Sl 3 sts to cn and hold to back, k3, k3 from cn.

C6F Sl 3 sts to cn and hold to front, k3, k3 from cn.

RT Right twist

Insert RH needle knitwise into second st on LH needle, knit without slipping st off needle, k first st, sl both sts off LH needle.

LT Left twist

Insert RH needle in back of second st on LH needle and k it, without slipping st off needle, k first st, then slip both sts off LH needle.

3-st RPC 3-st right purl twist

Sl 1 st to cn, hold to back, k2, p1 from cn.

3-st LPC 3-st left purl twist

Sl 2 sts to cn, hold to front, p1, k2 from cn.

4-st RC 4-st right cable

Sl 2 sts to cn, hold to back, k2, k2 from cn.

8-st RC 8-st right cable

Sl 4 sts to cn, hold to back, k4, k4 from cn.

4-St RC Sl 2 sts to cn and hold to back, k2, k2 from cn.

4-St LC Sl 2 sts to cn and hold to front, k2, k2 from cn.

4-St RPC Sl 2 sts to cn and hold to back, k2, p2 from cn.

Seed Stitch (over any number of sts).

Row 1 (RS) *K1, p1; rep from * to end.

Row 2 K the purl sts and p the knit sts. Rep row 2 for seed st.

MB Make Bobble

K into the front, back, front, back, front of next st, turn, k5, turn, p5, pass 4th, 3rd, 2nd and first st over the 5th st.

SHORT ROW SHAPING

(slip and wrap next st)

Knit side

1) Wyib, sl next st purlwise.

2) Move yarn between the needles to the front.

3) Sl the same st back to LH needle. Turn work, bring yarn to the p side between needles. One st is wrapped. To hide wraps when short rows are completed, work to just before wrapped st, insert RH needle under the wrap and knitwise into the wrapped st, k them tog.

Purl side

1) Wyif, sl next st purlwise.

2) Move yarn between the needles to the back of work.

3) Sl same st back to LH needle. Turn work, bring yarn back to the p side between the needles. One st is wrapped. To hide wraps when short rows are completed, work to just before wrapped st, insert RH needle from behind into the back lp of the wrap and place on LH needle; P wrap tog with st on needle.

YARN SYMBOLS	symbol	sts per 4"/10cm	weight
The following symbols 1-6 represent a range of stitch gauges. Note that these symbols respond to the standard gauge in stockinette stitch (over 4"/10cm).	①	29-32 sts	fine
	②	25-28 sts	light
	③	21-24 sts	medium
	④	17-20 sts	medium-heavy
	⑤	13-16 sts	bulky
	⑥	9-12 sts	extra-bulky

knitting terms and abbreviations

approx approximately

beg begin(ning)

bind off Used to finish an edge and keep stitches from unraveling. Lift the first stitch over the second, the second over the third, etc. (UK: cast off)

cast on A foundation row of stitches placed on the needle in order to begin knitting.

CC contrast color

ch chain(s)

cm centimeter(s)

cn cable needle

cont continu(e)(ing)

dc double crochet (UK: tr-treble)

dec decrease(ing)—Reduce the stitches in a row (knit 2 together).

dpn double pointed needle(s)

foll follow(s)(ing)

g gram(s)

garter stitch Knit every row. Circular knitting: knit one round, then purl one round.

hdc half-double crochet (UK: htr-half treble)

inc increase(ing)—Add stitches in a row (knit into the front and back of a stitch).

k knit

k2tog knit 2 stitches together

lp(s) loops(s)

LH left-hand

m meter(s)

M1 make one stitch—With the needle tip, lift the strand between last stitch worked and next stitch on the left-hand needle and knit into the back of it. One stitch has been added.

MC main color

mm millimeter(s)

oz ounce(s)

p purl

p2tog purl 2 stitches together

pat pattern

pick up and knit (purl) Knit (or purl) into the loops along an edge.

pm place marker—Place or attach a loop of contrast yarn or purchased stitch marker as indicated.

rem remain(s)(ing)

rep repeat

rev St st reverse Stockinette stitch—Purl right-side rows, knit wrong-side rows. Circular knitting: purl all rounds. (UK: reverse stocking stitch)

rnd(s) round(s)

RH right-hand

RS right side(s)

sc single crochet (UK: dc - double crochet)

sk skip

SKP Slip 1, knit 1, pass slip stitch over knit 1.

SK2P Slip 1, knit 2 together, pass slip stitch over k2tog.

sl slip—An unworked stitch made by passing a stitch from the left-hand to the right-hand needle as if to purl.

sl st slip stitch (UK: single crochet)

ssk slip, slip, knit—Slip next 2 stitches knitwise, one at a time, to right-hand needle. Insert tip of left-hand needle into fronts of these stitches from left to right. Knit them together. One stitch has been decreased.

st(s) stitch(es)

St st Stockinette stitch—Knit right-side rows, purl wrong-side rows. Circular knitting: knit all rounds. (UK: stocking stitch)

tbl through back of loop

tog together

tr treble crochet (UK: dtr-double treble)

WS wrong side(s)

w&t wrap and turn

wyif with yarn in front

wyib with yarn in back

work even Continue in pattern without increasing or decreasing. (UK: work straight)

yd yard(s)

yo yarn over—Make a new stitch by wrapping the yarn over the right-hand needle. (UK: yfwd, yon, yrn)

* Repeat directions following * as many times as indicated.

[ ] Repeat directions inside brackets as many times as indicated.

two-piece mosaic stole

(Continued from page 10)

A, p2, *sl 1 wyif, p3; rep from *, end sl 1 wyif, p2. **Row 3** With A, knit. **Row 4** With A, p2, * wrapping yarn twice around needle, p1, p 3; rep from *, end last rep p2 instead of p3. **Rows 5-8** With MC, rep rows 1-4. **Rows 9-12** With B, rep rows 1-4. **Rows 13-16** With MC, rep rows 1-4. **Rows 17-20** With C, rep rows 1-4. **Rows 21-24** With MC, rep rows 1-4. Rep these 24 rows for pat st until piece measures approx 54"/137cm from beg, ending with row 3 in MC.

Short edge trim

Next row (WS) With MC, *k3, k2tog, k4; rep from * 8 times more—72 sts. **Next row (RS)** Purl. **Next row (WS)** Knit. Bind off all sts purlwise.

Lengthwise trim

With RS facing, circular needle and MC, working along the left edge of the piece, pick up and k 1 st in every other row along side edge of piece to the trim, leave side of trim free. K1 row, p1 row, k1 row. Bind off all sts purlwise.

SHORT RECTANGLE

Work as for long rectangle until piece measures 36"/92cm. Work short-edge trim and left-side lengthwise trim as for long rectangle. Pin the cast-on edge of the short rectangle to the right side of the long rectangle underneath the trim (see diagram) stretching slightly. Sew this edge in place.

Final lengthwise trim

With RS facing, circular needle and MC, pick up and k 72 sts along the cast-on edge of the long rectangle then cont along the side edge of the short rectangle, picking up 1 st in every other row to lower edge. Work trim as for previous trims.

FINISHING

Block flat to measurements. Sew ends of trims tog at corners.

18"

SHORT
RECTANGLE

36"

36"

LONG
RECTANGLE

18"

54"

bobble-trimmed wrap shawl

(Continued from page 14)

from *, end k3, p3. **Row 6-8** K4, *p1, k7; rep from *, end p1, k4.

Row 9 Rep row 5. **Row 10** rep row 4. Rep rows 1-10 for pat.

WRAP

With CC, cast on 97 sts. **Row 1** *Make bobble (MB), k7; rep from *, end MB. **Rows 2 and 3** Knit. **Row 4** Change to MC, *k1, p1; rep from *, end k1. Beg fluted rib pat, cont until piece measures 70"/178cm from beg, end with a WS row. **Next row** Change to CC (do not cut MC), *k1, p1; rep from *, end k1. Knit the next 2 rows. **Next row** *MB, k1, psso (counts as first bind off), bind off 7 more sts; rep from *, end MB. Cut CC yarn, pull through.

FINISHING

Pick up MC, with crochet hook, work 1 row of rev sc along side edge, fasten off. Rep for other side. Block lightly.

trellis lace scarf

(Continued from page 16)

Beg trellis pat

Work 4 rows of trellis pat 6 times, end with row 3. Break yarn and sl sts to a holder.

Beg second layer

Rep from ** to **, then work 4 rows of trellis pat twice, end with row 3.

Attach layers

Next row With needles parallel, WS facing, and using 3rd needle, work row 4 of trellis pat, working sts tog from both needles. Cont on the one piece in trellis pat until piece measures 40"/101.5cm from beg, end with row 1 of pat. Place sts on a holder.

FINISHING

Graft the 2 pieces tog so that lace pat is in opposite directions. Steam lightly.

fringed geometric wrap

(Continued from page 18)

Embellishments

Crochet embellishments are worked free form. You can create zig zag, straight or curved lines as foll: position square so tails are at RH side. From RS with hook and color 1 tail, make a slip knot at base of tail and place on hook. Working on color 2 side, ch 3, sl st in a st, *ch 3, sl st in desired st; rep from * until a 3"/7.5cm tail rem, or you have completed desired design. Fasten off. Using color 2 tail, embellish color 1 side.

FINISHING

Sew squares tog foll placement diagram so that embellishments are at top left corner.

Edging

With RS facing and hook, join C with a sl st in top right corner. Making sure that work lies flat, sc evenly around entire edge, changing colors to match colors of squares and working 3 sc in each corner. Join rnd with a sl st in first sc. Ch 1, turn to WS. **Fringe row** *Ch 40, sl st in next st, sc in next st; rep from * across right side edge, bottom edge and left side edge, changing colors to match colors of squares. Ch 1, turn to RS. **Top edge** Working from left to right, sc in each st across, changing colors to match colors of squares. Fasten off.

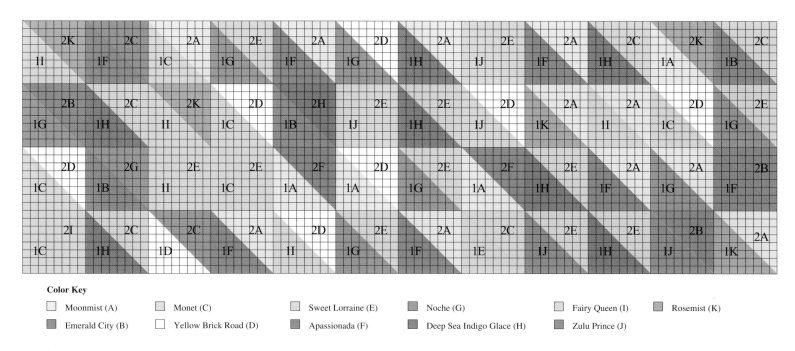

Color Key

- Moonmist (A)
- Emerald City (B)
- Monet (C)
- Yellow Brick Road (D)
- Sweet Lorraine (E)
- Apassionada (F)
- Noche (G)
- Deep Sea Indigo Glace (H)
- Fairy Queen (I)
- Zulu Prince (J)
- Rosemist (K)

summer lace shawl

(Continued from page 20)

p2tog] twice, yo, k3, [p1, k1] in last st. Turn. K1, yo, k2, yo, p2tog. Turn. Yo, p2tog, yo, k3, [p1, k1] in last st. **Row 6** Bind off 5 sts (1 st rem on RH needle), yo, p2tog, k1, [yo, p2tog] twice, k4, [yo, p2tog] 3 times, k4. **Row 7** Sl 1, k3, [yo, p2tog] twice, yo, ssk, k4, [yo, p2tog] twice, [p1, k1] in next st, yo, p2tog, yo, [p1, k1] in last st. *Turn. K3, yo, p2tog. Turn. Yo, p2tog, yo, k2, yo, [p1, k1] in last st.* **Row 8** Bind off 5 sts, yo, p2tog, yo, k2, [yo, p2tog] twice, k3, p2tog tbl, yo, k1, [yo, p2tog] twice, k4. **Row 9** Sl 1, k3, [yo, p2tog] twice, k2, yo, ssk, k2, [yo, p2tog] twice, k2, [p1, k1] in next st, yo, p2tog, yo, [p1, k1] in last st; rep between *'s of row 7. **Row 10** Bind off 5 sts, yo, p2tog, yo, k4, [yo, p2tog] twice, k1, p2tog tbl, yo, k3, [yo, p2tog] twice, k4. **Row 11** Sl 1, k3, [yo, p2tog] twice, k4, yo, ssk, [yo, p2tog] twice, k4, [p1, k1] in next st, yo, p2tog, yo, [p1, k1] in last st; rep between *'s of row 7. **Row 12** Bind off 5 sts, yo, p2tog, yo, k6, [yo, p2tog] 3 times, k4, [yo, p2tog] twice, k4. **Row 13** Sl 1, k3, [yo, p2tog] twice, k3, k2tog, yo, k1, [yo, p2tog] twice, k6, [p1, k1] in next st, yo, p2tog, yo, [p1, k1] in last st; rep between *'s of row 7. **Row 14** Bind off 5 sts, yo, p2tog, yo, k8, [yo, p2tog] twice, k2, yo, p2tog, k2, [yo, p2tog] twice, k4. **Row 15** Sl 1, k3, [yo, p2tog] twice, k1, k2tog, yo, k3, [yo, p2tog] twice, k8, [p1, k1] in next st, yo, p2tog, yo, [p1, k1] in last st; rep between *'s of row 7. **Row 16** Bind off 5 sts, yo, p2tog, yo, p3tog, k7, [yo, p2tog] twice, k4, [yo, p2tog] 3 times, k4. **Row 17** Sl 1, k3, [yo, p2tog] twice, yo, ssk, k4, [yo, p2tog] twice, k6, k2tog, k1, yo, p2tog, yo, [p1, k1] in last st; rep between *'s of row 7. **Row 18** Bind off 5 sts, yo, p2tog, yo, p3tog, k5, [yo, p2tog] twice, k3, p2tog tbl, yo, k1, [yo, p2tog] twice, k4. **Row 19** Sl 1, k3, [yo, p2tog] twice, k2, yo, ssk, k2, [yo, p2tog] twice, k4, k2tog, k1, yo, p2tog, yo, [p1, k1] in last st; rep between *'s of row 7. **Row 20** Bind off 5 sts, yo, p2tog, yo, p3tog, k3, [yo, p2tog] twice, k1, p2tog tbl, yo, k3, [yo, p2tog] twice, k4. **Row 21** Sl 1, k3, [yo, p2tog] twice, k4, yo, ssk, [yo, p2tog] twice, k2, k2tog, k1, yo, p2tog, yo, [p1, k1] in last st; rep between *'s of row 7. **Row 22** Bind off 5 sts, yo, p2tog, yo, p3tog, k1, [yo, p2tog] 3 times, k4, [yo, p2tog] twice, k4. **Row 23** Sl 1, k3, [yo, p2tog] twice, k3, k2tog, yo, k1, [yo, p2tog] twice, k2tog, k1, yo, p2tog, yo, [p1, k1] in last st; rep between *'s of row 7. **Row 24** Bind off 5 sts, yo, [p2tog] twice, [yo, p2tog] twice, k2, yo, p2tog, k2, [yo, p2tog] twice, k4. **Row 25** Sl 1, k3, [yo, p2tog] twice, k1, k2tog, yo, k3, [yo, p2tog] twice, SK2P, k1. **Row 26** K2tog, [yo, p2tog] twice, k4, [yo, p2tog] 3 times, k4. **Row 27** Sl 1, k3, [yo, p2tog] twice, yo, ssk, k4, [yo, p2tog] twice, k1. **Row 28** K1, [yo, p2tog] twice, k3, p2tog tbl, yo, k1, [yo, p2tog] twice, k4. **Row 29** Sl 1, k3, [yo, p2tog] twice, k2, yo, ssk, k2, [yo, p2tog] twice, k1. **Row 30** K1, [yo, p2tog] twice, k1, p2tog tbl, yo, k3, [yo, p2tog] twice, k4. Rep rows 1-30 for Chart II.

Note: Work shawl decs 1 st in from each side edge, making adjustments to Chart I pat as necessary to maintain correct st count. Bind off when decreasing more than one st at a time. Shawl directions indicate the number of sts that should be decreased at each side on a given row.

SHAWL

With circular needle, cast on 277 sts. K 6 rows. Work Chart I, AT SAME TIME, dec 1 st each side as foll: on 11th row, then foll 6th row once, 5th row once, 4th row once, then every 3rd row 10 times, every other row twice, [on next row, then on alternate row] 7 times, every row 11 times. Cont dec or binding off each side on every row as foll: [2 sts once, then 1 st once] 4 times, 1 st twice, [2 sts once, then 1 st once] 3 times, [3 sts once, then 1 st once] 5 times, [4 sts once, then 1 st once] twice, [5 sts once, then 1 st once] 3 times, 5 sts once (130 total chart rows). Bind off rem 43 sts.

Edging

With RS facing and garter st border at lower edge, tip up lower LH corner of shawl and with dpn pick up and p5 sts along WS of garter st border rows, leave yarn. With circular needle and separate skein, cast on 19 sts. **Next row (WS)** K18, then holding needles parallel, k last st on circular needle tog with first picked-up st on dpn. Turn. **Next row (RS)** Wyib, sl 1 st from dpn to circular needle, k2tog, k to end. K 3 more rows, joining sts as before on every row. Turn.

Beg Chart II

Next row (RS) Work row 1 of Chart II over 19 sts on circular needle. Measure around shawl and place a yarn marker every 4"/10cm (omitting garter st rows at end). With dpn and yarn left from picking up sts, pick up and p15 sts (from WS) between last row worked and next marker. Work chart row 2, k last st of chart tog with 1 st from dpn. Turn. Work chart row 3 (do not join sts). Cont working Chart II over sts on circular needle, knitting tog the last st of each WS row tog with 1 st on dpn. 30 rows of chart will be worked between each pair of markers. Work until 30 rows of chart have been worked 17 times, picking up 15 sts along edge for each 30-row rep of chart. Pick up and p 6 sts along garter rows. K 6 rows, joining edging to shawl on every row as before, binding off all sts on last row.

FINISHING

Dampen shawl and pin to size, placing 1 pin in each point around edging. Let dry completely.

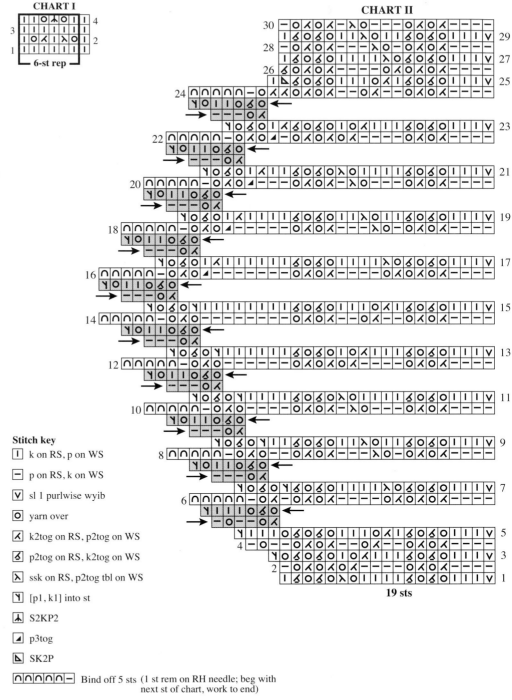

CHART I

CHART II

Stitch key

- ☐ k on RS, p on WS
- ☐ p on RS, k on WS
- V sl 1 purlwise wyib
- O yarn over
- ☒ k2tog on RS, p2tog on WS
- ☒ p2tog on RS, k2tog on WS
- ☒ ssk on RS, p2tog tbl on WS
- ☒ [p1, k1] into st
- ☒ S2KP2
- ☒ p3tog
- ☒ SK2P

∩∩∩∩∩☐ Bind off 5 sts (1 st rem on RH needle; beg with next st of chart, work to end)

Note: On shaded rows: work in direction of arrow over ☐ sts in shaded boxes only, turn, work next shaded row.

chevron stripe wrap

(Continued from page 24)

LEFT FRONT

Rejoin yarn to sts on holder and complete as for right front, foll last 72 sts of chart.

FINISHING

Block to measurements.

Front edging

With circular needle and B, pick up and k 136 sts evenly along inside edge of right front and 136 sts along inside edge of left front. K 1 row. Change to A and k 2 rows. Bind off.

Side edgings

With circular needle and B, pick up and k 136 sts evenly along side edge of left front and 128 sts along side edge of back. K 1 row. Change to A and k 2 rows. Bind off. Work to correspond along other side.

Color Key

- ☐ Black (A)
- ☐ Mauve (B)
- ☐ Med blue (C)
- ☐ Forest green (D)
- ☐ Navy (E)
- ☐ Purple (F)
- ☐ Burgundy (G)
- ☐ Rust (H)
- ☐ Brown (I)
- ☐ Olive green (J)

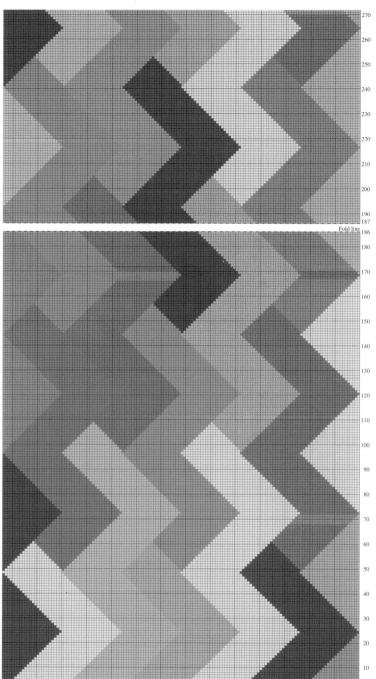

winter shrug

(Continued from page 26)

are 119 sts. Work even until piece measures 19½"/49.5cm from beg. Place a marker each end of row for end of sleeve. Work even until piece measures 21"/53cm above marker. Place another marker each end of row for beg of next sleeve. Work 3½"/9cm more, then dec 1 st each side on next row, then alternately every 2nd and 4th row until there are 53 sts. Work even until piece measures 15½"/39.5cm from last marker. Change to smaller needles and work in k1, p1 rib, dec 4 sts evenly across first row—49 sts. When rib measures 4"/10 cm, bind off in rib.

FINISHING

Block piece to measurements. Sew sleeve seams at markers.

(Schematic diagram labeled: SLEEVE, BODY, SLEEVE with measurements: 4", 15½", 21", 3½", 12", 4", 10", 22")

wave pattern wrap

(Continued from page 28)

WAVE PATTERN (multiple of 10 sts plus 6)

Rows 1 and 2 Knit. **Row 3** K6, *(yo) once, k1, (yo) twice, k1, (yo) 3 times, k1, (yo) twice, k1, (yo) once, k6; rep from * to end. **Row 4** K, dropping all yos. **Rows 5 and 6** Knit. **Row 7** K1; rep from * of row 3, end k1 instead of k6. **Row 8** Rep row 4. Rep rows 1-8 for wave pat.

WRAP

Cast on 56 sts with desired color. Work in wave pat, using colors and yarns as desired, for 80"/203cm, or desired length. Bind off.

FINISHING

Weave in ends. Block to measurements.

turtleneck capelet

(Continued from page 32)

Shoulder shaping

Rep dec rnd 3 every rnd a total of 8 times—34 sts. **Next rnd** *K1, p1; rep from * around. Rep this rnd for k1, p1 rib for 4½"/11.5cm. Bind off in rib.

FINISHING

Lay work flat and steam very lightly to finished measurements.

tweed poncho

(Continued from page 34)

Rep last 2 rnds 5 times more, working one more k st before and after every yo, k1, yo, every other rnd.

Remove 2nd and 4th markers (at shoulders). Cont working yo, k1, yo every other rnd at center back and front only, working rem sts as knit, for 74 rows (or 37 eyelets after shoulder eyelets). Piece should measure approx 22"/56cm from last shoulder eyelets. Bind off all sts.

FRINGE

Using 3 strands for each fringe, attach fringe (4"/10cm finished length) along lower edge of poncho (see photo).

cowl neck poncho

(Continued from page 36)

BACK

Cast on 120 (144, 162) sts. Work in seed st for 6 rows. **Twist row (RS)** Cont in seed st, work 6 sts, *rotate LH needle counterclockwise 360°, work next 6 sts; rep from * to end. Cont in seed st until piece measures 28 (30, 32)"/71 (76, 81.5)cm from beg, end with a WS row. **Next row (RS)** Work across 48 (60, 67) sts and place on holder for right shoulder, bind off center 24 (24, 28) sts, work rem 48 (60, 67) sts and place on holder for left shoulder.

FRONT

Work as for back until piece measures 26 (28, 30)"/66 (71, 76)cm from beg, end with a WS row.

Neck shaping

Next row (RS) Work 50 (62, 70) sts, join a 2nd ball of yarn and bind off center 20 (20, 22) sts, work to end. Working both sides at once, dec 1 st at each neck edge every other row 2 (2, 3) times—48 (60, 67) sts each side. Work even until piece measures same length as back to shoulders. Place sts each side on holders.

FINISHING

Join shoulders, using 3-needle bind-off.

Collar

Cast on 74 (74, 80) sts. Work in seed st for 6 rows. **Twist row (RS)** Cont in seed st, work 4 sts, *rotate LH needle counterclockwise 360°, work next 6 sts; rep from *, end last rep work 4 sts. Cont in seed st until collar measures 10"/25.5cm from beg. Bind off. Sew seam. Sew bound-off edge of collar evenly around neck edge.

Tassels (make 4)

Cast on 10 sts, Work in seed st for 2½"/6.5cm, end with a WS row. **Next row (RS)** Bind off 5 sts and fasten off st rem on RH needle. Remove 4 sts from LH needle and unravel them down to cast-on edge. Fasten off last st on cast-on row. Sew bound-off and cast-on edges tog. With tapestry needle, run single strand through sts along top of tassel and gather tog tightly. Stuff top of tassel with fiberfill, forming a ball.

Tie

Cast on 8 sts. Work 1 row in Seed st. Bind off in pat. Sew tie around tassel under fiberfill and secure. Trim ends of fringe. Sew tassels to lower corners of poncho.

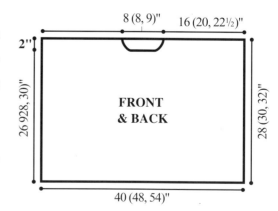

turtleneck poncho

(Continued from page 40)

k2tog, k69, k2tog tbl, pm, k1, k2tog, k29—133 sts. **Next row** Purl. **Next (dec) row** (RS) Work to within 2 sts of marker, k2tog tbl, k1, k2tog, k to within 2 sts of marker, k2tog tbl, k1, k2tog, work to end—129 sts. Cont as established, working dec row every other row 17 times more, every 4th row 10 times—21 sts. P 1 row. Bind off all sts.

FRONT

Cast on 137 sts. K 1 row. **Next row (WS)** K61, M1, k1, M1, k3, M1, k2, M1, k3, M1, k2, M1, k3, M1, k1, M1, k61—145 sts.

Beg cable pat

Next row (RS) Work 60 sts, work row 1 of cable pat over next 25 sts, work to end. Cont as established, working 16 row cable pat over center 25 sts, AT SAME TIME, when piece measures 1½"/4cm, work dec's as for back. Cont until piece measures same as back. Bind off all sts, dec 8 sts evenly across cable pat on bind off row.

FINISHING

Sew right seam.

Turtleneck

With RS facing, pick up and k42 sts evenly around neck edge. **Next row (WS)** K2, *p2, k2; rep from * to end. **Next row** K the knit and p the purl sts. Rep last 2 rows until rib measures 4"/10cm from beg, end with a RS row. **Next row (WS)** K1, M1, k1, *p2, k1, M1, k1; rep from * to end—53 sts. **Next row (RS)** P3, *k2, p3; rcp from * to end. **Next row** K the knit and P the purl sts. Rep last 2 rows until rib measures 8"/20cm from beg. Bind off in rib.

Sew left side seam and collar, reversing seam for top 4"/10cm for turnback.

Fringe

Cut 30"/76cm lengths of yarn and holding 3 strands together, place fringe through each st around lower edge of poncho.

aran poncho

(Continued from page 42)

BACK

With scrap yarn cast on 53 sts. Work a few rows St st, end with a WS row. Change to 2 strands MC held tog. **Foundation Row (WS)** K3, p8, k4, p2, [k2, p4] 3 times, k2, p8, k4, p2, k2.

Beg Chart

Next row Beg chart row 1. Cont to work chart, cast on 2 sts at beg of row 3, 5 and 7, and 6 sts at beg of row 9 as indicated (for shoulder shaping)—65 sts. Cont to work chart pat through row 27, then, work 22 rows of short row shaping as foll:

Next row (WS) Work to last 7 sts, sl and wrap next st, turn. **Next row (RS)** Cont over 58 sts in pats as established. **Next row (WS)** Work to last st, sl and wrap next st, turn. **Next row (RS)** Cont over 57 sts in pats as established. **Next row (WS)** Work to last 5 sts, sl and wrap next st, turn. **Next row (RS)** Cont over 52 sts in pats as established. **Next row (WS)** Work to last st, sl and wrap next st, turn. **Next row (RS)** Cont over 51 sts in pats as established. **Next row (WS)** Work to last 5 sts, sl and wrap next st, turn. **Next row (RS)** Cont over 46 sts in pats as established. **Next row (WS)** Work to last st, sl and wrap next st, turn. **Next row (RS)** Cont over 45 sts in pats as established. **Next row (WS)** Work to last 9 sts, sl and wrap next st, turn. **Next row (RS)** Cont over 36 sts in pats as established. **Next row (WS)** Work to last st, sl and wrap next st, turn. **Next row (RS)** Cont over 35 sts in pats as established. **Next row (WS)** Work to last 5 sts, sl and wrap next st, turn. **Next row (RS)** Cont over 30 sts in pats as established. **Next row (WS)** Work to last 6 sts, sl and wrap next st, turn. **Next row (RS)** Cont over 24 sts in pats as established. **Next row (WS)** Work to last 12 sts, sl and wrap next st, turn. **Next row (RS)** Cont over 12 sts in pats as established. **Next row (WS)** Work across all sts, knitting short-row wraps tog with wrapped st to hide (as per glossary). **Next row (RS)** Center neck row work across all sts (Note: this should be cross row for 4-st cable and bobble row for zigzag pat). **Next row (WS)** Work 12 sts, sl and wrap next st, turn. **Next row (RS)** Work to end in pats as established. **Next row (WS)** Work 24 sts. **Next row (RS)** Work to end in pats as established. **Next row (WS)** Work 30 sts. **Next row (RS)** Work to end in pats as established. Cont to reverse short row shaping until all sts have been worked. Cont in pat as established for 18 rows. Bind off 6 sts at beg of next RS row, then 3 sts three times (shoulder shaping). Work 2 rows. Change to scrap yarn. Bind off.

FRONT

Work as for back.

FINISHING

Block lightly with steam. With tapestry needle, 2 strands MC held tog and RS facing, use Kitchener St to graft tog pieces at side. Unravel and discard scrap yarn. Sew tog cast on and bind off sts at shoulder.

Fringe

With crochet hook, and 2 strands held tog, beg at side seam, with WS facing, work along lower edge of poncho as foll: *work 4 sl st, ch10, sk 2 ch and work sl st into rem 8 ch. Rep from * around.

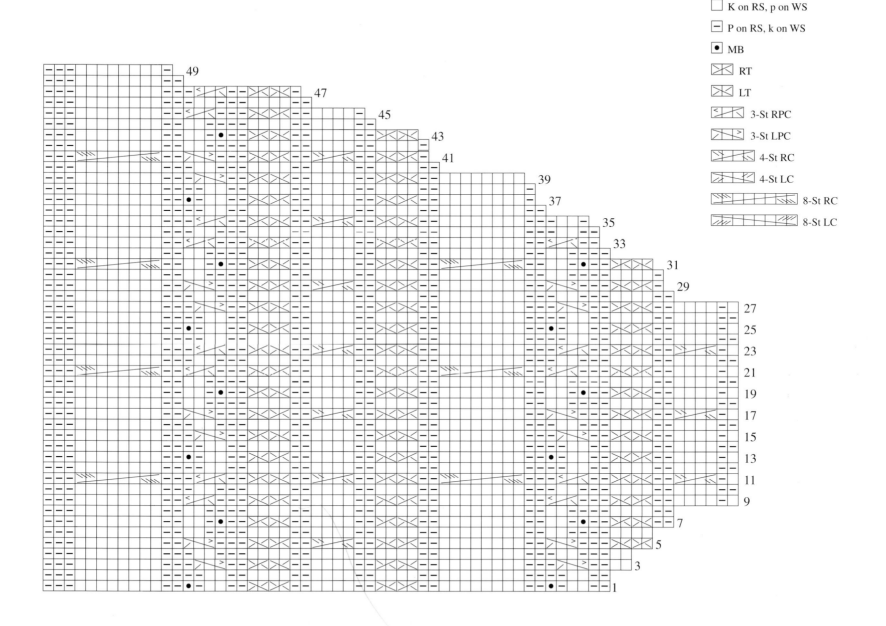

Stitch Key

☐ K on RS, p on WS

– P on RS, k on WS

• MB

⧓ RT

⧓ LT

3-St RPC

3-St LPC

4-St RC

4-St LC

8-St RC

8-St LC

mock turtleneck poncho

(Continued from page 44)

Shoulder and neck shaping

Bind off 4 sts at beg of next 14 rows, 5 sts at beg of next 24 rows, AT SAME TIME, when piece measures 20½"/52cm from beg, shape neck as foll: Work to center 18 sts, join a 2nd ball of yarn and bind off center 18 sts, work to end. Working both sides at once, bind off from each neck edge 2 sts once, 1 st once.

FRONT

Work as for back until piece measures 18½"/47cm from beg.

Neck shaping

Next row (RS) Cont shoulder shaping as for back, AT SAME TIME, work to center 10 sts, join a 2nd ball of yarn and bind off center 10 sts, work to end. Working both sides at once, bind off from each neck edge 3 sts once, 2 sts once, 1 st twice.

FINISHING

Block pieces to measurements. Sew top seams.

Mock turtleneck

With shorter circular needle, pick up and k 67 sts evenly around neck edge. Join and place marker for beg of rnd. Work ridge pat in rnds for 6 rnds. Dec 6 sts evenly across next rnd—61 sts. Work even in ridge pat for 3 rnds. Dec 7 sts evenly across next rnd—54 sts. Work even in ridge pat for 17 rnds. Bind off loosely purlwise.

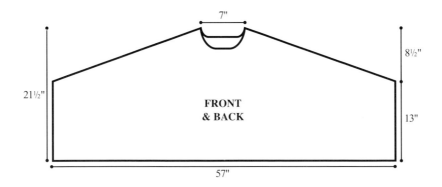

spiral lace capelet

(Continued from page 46)

CAPELET

Beg at lower edge with double strand of yarn and larger circular needle, cast on 165 sts. Join and work in rnds. Place marker at beg of rnd. [K 1 rnd, p 1 rnd] 3 times. K 1 rnd.

Beg pat st

Rnd 1 *SKP, k6, yo, p3; rep from * around. Rnd 2 *K8, p3; rep from * around. Rep these 2 rnds 7 times more. Dec rnd 1 *SKP, k6, p3, rep from * around. Next rnd *K7, p3; rep from * around. Next rnd *SKP, k5, yo, p3; rep from * around. Next rnd *K7, p3; rep from * around. Rep last 2 rnds twice more. Dec rnd 2 *SKP, k5, p3; rep from * around. Next rnd *K6, p3; rep from * around. Next rnd *SKP, k4, yo, p3; rep from * around. Next rnd *K6, p3, rep from * around. Rep last 2 rnds twice more. Cont to dec in this way every 8th rnd, (by eliminating yo then having 1 less k st on next rnd), 3 times more—90 sts. Change to smaller circular needle. Next rnd *K3, p3, rep from * around. Cont in k3, p3 rib for 6"/15cm. [K 1 rnd, p 1 rnd] twice. Bind off knitwise. Do not press or block.

HAT

With double strand of yarn and smaller circular needle, cast on 66 sts. K 1 rnd, p 1 rnd, k 1 rnd.

Beg pat st

Rnd 1 *SKP, k6, yo, p3; rep from * around. Rnd 2 *K8, p3; rep from * around. Rep these 2 rnds 17 times more. Dec rnd 1 *SKP, k6, p3; rep from * around—60 sts. Next rnd *K7, p3; rep from * around. Next rnd *SKP, k5, yo, p3; rep from * around. Next rnd *K7, p3; rep from * around. Rep last 2 rnds twice more. Dec rnd 2 *SKP, k5, p3; rep from * around—54 sts. Next rnd *K6, p3; rep from * around. Next rnd *SKP, k4, yo, p3; rep from * around. Next rnd *K6, p3; rep from * around. Rep last 2 rnds twice more. Next rnd *K2tog, rep from * around—27 sts. K 3 rnds. With dpn, [k2tog] 13 times, k1. Pull yarn through rem sts and draw up tightly and fasten off. Do not press or block.

seed stitch cap

(Continued from page 50)

*Work 5 sts seed st, k2tog; rep from * to end—36 sts. Next rnd *Work 5 sts seed st, k1; rep from * to end. Next rnd *Work 4 sts seed st, k2tog; rep from * to end—30 sts. Next rnd *Work 4 sts seed st, k1; rep from * to end. Next rnd *Work 3 sts seed st, k2tog; rep from * to end—24 sts. Next rnd *Work 2 sts seed st, k2tog; rep from * to end—18 sts. Next rnd *Work 1 st seed st, k2tog; rep from * to end—12 sts. Rep last rnd once more—6 sts. Next rnd K2tog across.

FINISHING

Pull yarn through rem 3 sts. With crochet hook and B, ch 50 sts. Turn and sl st into every ch. Fold chain in half and attach center of chain to top of hat. Make 2 pompoms and attach to each end of chain.

diamond scarf

(Continued from page 52)

Rows 13, 15, 17 and 19 (RS) With G2, k8, with S1, k8, with G3, k8. **Row 20** With G3, k8, with S1, p8, with G2, k8, with G4, cast on 8 sts—32 sts. **Row 21** (RS) With G4, k8, with S2, k8, with G5, k8, with S3, k8, with G6, cast on 8 sts—40 sts. **Rows 22, 24, 26, 28 and 30** With G6, k8, with S3, p8, with G5, k8, with S2, p8, with G4, k8. **Rows 23, 25, 27 and 29 (RS)** With G4, k8, with S2, k8, with G5, k8, with S3, k8, with G6, cast on 8 sts—40 sts. **Row 31 (RS)** With G4, bind off 8 sts, with G7, k8, with S4, k8, with G8, k8, with S5, k8, with G1, cast on 8 sts. **Rows 32, 34, 36, 38 and 40** With G1, k8, with S5, p8, with G8, k8, with S4, p8, with G7, k8. **Rows 33, 35, 37 and 39 (RS)** With G7, k8, with S4, k8, with G8, k8, with S5, k8, with G1, k8. **Row 41 (RS)** With G7, bind off 8 sts, with G2, k8, with S6, k8, with G3, k8, with S7, k8, with G4, cast on 8 sts. **Rows 42, 44, 46, 48 and 50** With G4, k8, with S7, p8, with G3, k8, with S6, p8, with G2, k8. **Rows 43, 45, 47 and 49 (RS)** With G2, k8, with S6, k8, with G3, k8, with S7, k8, with G4, k8. Keeping to color sequence as established, rep rows 41 to 50 12 times more, then rows 41-49 once. **Row 190 (WS)** With G6, bind off 8 sts, with S3, p8, with G5, k8, with S2, p8, with G4, k8—32 sts. **Row 191** With G4, bind off 8 sts, with G7, k8, with S4, k8, with G8, k8—24 sts. **Rows 192, 194, 196 and 198** With G8 k8, with S4, p8, with G7, k8. **Rows 193, 195, 197 and 199** With G7 k8, with S4, k8, with G8, k8. **Row 200 (WS)** With G8, bind off 8 sts, with S4, p8, with G7, k8—16 sts. **Row 201** With G7, bind off 8 sts, with G1, k8—8 sts. **Rows 202-210** Knit. Bind off knitwise.

FINISHING

Block lightly to measurements.

Tassels (make 6)

Make 4"/10cm long tassels. Sew a tassel to each point at each end scarf as shown.

lace-pattern scarf

(Continued from page 56)

Row 3 [K1, p1] twice, [k1tbl, p1] twice, p2, k5, SKP, p2, [k1tbl, p1] twice, [p1, yo] twice, p2, [k1tbl, p1] twice, p1, k2tog, k5, p3, [k1tbl, p1]twice, k1, p1, k1.

Row 4 [P1, k1] twice, [p1tbl, k1] twice, k2, p6, k2, [p1tbl, k1] twice, [k1, p1] twice, k2, [p1tbl, k1] twice, k1, p6, k3, [p1tbl, k1] twice, p1, k1, p1.

Rep rows 1 and 2 once more. Bind off in pat.

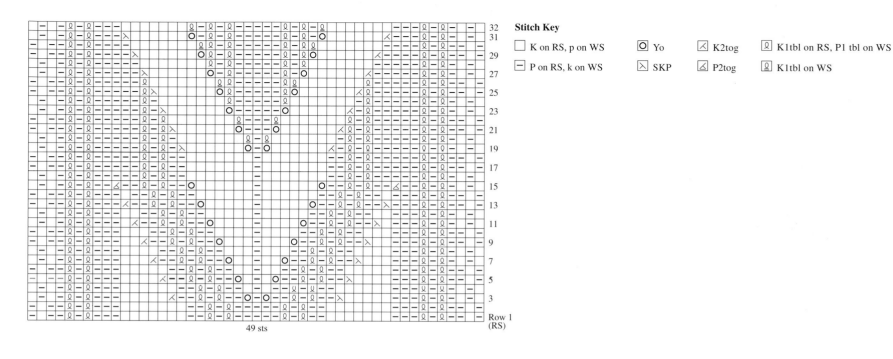

Row numbers right side: 32, 31, 29, 27, 25, 23, 21, 19, 17, 15, 13, 11, 9, 7, 5, 3, Row 1 (RS)

49 sts

Stitch Key

☐ K on RS, p on WS   ◯ Yo   ⟋ K2tog   Ω K1tbl on RS, P1 tbl on WS

— P on RS, k on WS   ⟍ SKP   ⟍ P2tog   Ω K1tbl on WS

FINISHING

Block lightly.

multi-pink scarf

(Continued from page 58)

Row 2 With B, work 4 sts in seed st, beg chart with st 24, p to st 1, with A, work seed st to end. Cont in pats as established through row 28. **Next row (RS)** With A, work 4 sts in seed st, join another ball of yarn and work row 1 of chart, with B, work in seed st to end. Cont as established until scarf measures approx 55"/139.5cm from beg, end with a WS row.

Beg chart 2

Work as for chart 1 through row 28.

Next row (RS) With A, work in seed st for 4 rows.

Bind off in seed st.

Color Key

☐ Orange (C)   ☐ Pink (G)

■ Burgundy (D)   ☐ Purple (H)

■ Periwinkle (E)   ■ Plum (I)

■ Magenta (F)   ■ Grey/burgundy heather (J)

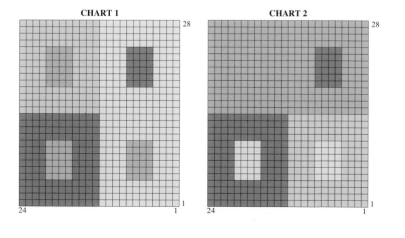

CHART 1   CHART 2

head into the cold   **133**

ribbed hooded cowl

(Continued from page 60)

Pompoms (make 7)

Cut two 2"/5cm cardboard circles. Cut hole in center approx ⅓ the size of circle. Cut ½"/1.5cm piece of circle away for easier wrapping of yarn. Place circles tog and wrap yarn thickly around circles. Insert scissors between cardboards and carefully cut around pompom. Cut a doubled strand and insert between cardboards. Tie tightly. Remove cardboards and trim pompom. Attach evenly around cast-on edge.

aran scarf with knotted fringe

(Continued from page 66)

Rows 1, 3 and 7 (RS) Knit. **Rows 2, 4, 6 and 8** Purl. **Row 5** Sl 3 sts to cn and hold to front, k3, k3 from cn. Rep rows 1-8 for 6-st left cable pat.

SCARF

With smaller needles and 2 strands of yarn held tog, cast on 48 sts. P 1 row on WS. **Next row (RS)** P14, M1, p3, M1, p5, M1, p5, M1, p5, M1, p7, M1, p9—54 sts. Change to larger needles. **Next row** K9, p6, k4, p4, k2, p4, k2, p4, k4, p6, k9. Beg pats **Next row (RS)** Work 7 sts sand st, 2 sts rev St st, row 1 of 6-st right cable pat, 2 sts rev St st, row 1 of aran braid chart, 2 sts rev St st, row 1 of 6-st left cable pat, 2 sts rev St st, 7 sts sand st. Cont in pats as established until piece measures 90"/228.5cm from beg, end with row 16 of aran braid chart. Change to smaller needles. **Next row** (RS) K9, k2tog, k2, k2tog, k5, k2tog, k4, k2tog, k4, k2tog, k5, k2tog, k2, k2tog, k9—47 sts. Bind off.

FINISHING

With crochet hook and 2 strands of yarn held together, work 48 sc across short edge of scarf, turn. **Next row** *3 sc, ch 2, skip 2 sc; rep from *, end 3 sc. Make 9 fringes and place in each ch-2 space. Trim fringe evenly. Rep on other short edge.

ARAN BRAID CHART

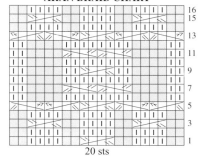

20 sts

Stitch Key

☐ K on RS, p on WS	4-st RC
☐ P on RS, k on WS	4-st RPC
4-st LC	4 st LPC

cabled helmut hat

(Continued from page 68)

HAT

With circular needle and with 2 strands of yarn from 2nd earflap, sl 15 earflap sts to circular needle; then cast on 22 sts for center front, cut yarn, sl 15 earflap sts of 2nd earflap to circular needle; with long end, cast on 14 sts for center back—66 sts. Cut yarn and slide last 7 cast-on sts to other end of needle and rejoin 2 strands of yarn to the next 7 cast-on sts (this is center back). Be sure that sts do not twist on needle and pm to mark beg of rnd. **Rnd 1** P7, k15 (earflap), p5, k12, p5, k15 (earflap), p7. **Rnd 2** K25, p2, k12, p2, k25. **Rnds 3 and 4** Rep rnd 2. **Rnd 5** Inc 1 st in first st, work even to last st, inc 1 st in last st—68 sts. **Rnd 6** Work even as established. **Rnd 7** K26, p2, sl next 6 sts to cn and hold to front, k6, k6 from cn, p2, k26. **Rnds 8-16** Work even as established. **Rnd 17** K26, p2, sl next 6 sts to cn and hold to front, k2, k2tog, k2, then k2, k2tog, k2 from cn (for 10-st cable), p2, k26—66 sts. **Rnds 18-21** Work even as established. **Rnd 22** K1, k2tog, k19, SKP, k2, p2, k10, p2, k2, k2tog, k19, SKP, k1. **Rnd 23** K1, k2tog, k17, SKP, k2, p2, k10, p2, k2, k2tog, k17, SKP, k1. **Rnd 24** K1, k2tog, k15, SKP, k2, p2tog, sl next 5 sts to cn and hold to front, k2, k2tog, k1, then k2, k2tog, k1 from cn (for 8-st cable), p2tog, k2, k2tog, k15, SKP, k1—50 sts. Divide sts onto 3 dpn, having 18 sts on needle 1, 14 sts on needle 2 and 18 sts on needle 3. **Rnds 25-29** Cont to dec 4 sts as before, with decs at beg and end of needles 1 and 3 as established (there are 2 sts less between these 2 decs on each needle) and working needle 2 sts even. **Rnd 30** Dec 4 sts as before, work the center 8 cable sts as foll: sl 4 sts to cn and hold to front, k1, k2tog, k1, then k1, k2tog, k1 from cn (for 6-st cable)—24 sts at completion of rnd. **Rnd 31** Work 4 decs as before—20 sts. **Rnd 32** K4, SKP, k2tog, k4, SKP, k2tog, k4—16 sts. **Rnd 33** K2tog, SKP, k2tog, k4, SKP, k2tog, SKP—10 sts. **Rnd 34** [K2tog] 5 times. Pull yarn through rem 5 sts, draw up tightly and secure. Cut yarn leaving a long end.

TASSEL

Wind yarn 28 times around a 5"/12.5cm cardboard. Cut at one end and secure looped end ¾"/2cm from top with one of the ends, winding around several times. Secure tassel at top of hat with end from hat.

TWISTED CORDS (make 2)

Fold 2 lengths of 60"/152cm each in half and make twisted cords. Knot and fringe for end. Attach cords to earflaps.

geometric scarf

(Continued from page 70)

SCARF

Work 11 squares, in color rnds as foll:

Square 1 4 B, 4 MC, 4 A, 4 MC, 4 D, 4 MC, 4 C. **Squares 2 and 8** [4A, 4MC] 3 times, 4A. **Square 3** 4 C, 4 MC, 4 D, 4 MC, 4 B, 4 MC, 4A. **Squares 4 and 10** [4B, 4MC] 3 times, 4B. **Square 5** 4 A, 4 MC, 4 B, 4 MC, 4 C, 4 MC, 4 D. **Square 6** [4C, 4MC] 3 Times, 4C. **Square 7** 4 D, 4 MC, 4 A, 4 MC, 4 C, 4 MC, 4 B. **Square 9** 4 C, 4 MC, 4 A, 4 MC, 4 D, 4 MC, 4 B. **Square 11** 4 A, 4 MC, 4 C, 4 MC, 4 B, 4 MC, 4 D.

FINISHING

With MC, join squares on 1 side in numerical order.

Edging

With circular needle, pick up 1 st in each cast on st along one long edge of scarf. Working back and forth, k 2 rows. Bind off. Rep for other long edge and both short edges.

seed stitch hat and scarf

(Continued from page 72)

Brim

Note: Brim is worked horizontally. **Row 1 (WS)** K3, *p2, k2; rep from * to end. **Row 2** *P2, k2; rep from *, end p3. Mark end of last row for top edge of brim. Rep rows 1 and 2 for rib pat and work even until piece measures 19½"/49.5cm from beg, end with row 2. Bind off in rib pat.

Crown

With RS of brim facing, pick up and k 51 sts evenly spaced along top edge. Work in seed st for 3 rows.

Crown shaping

Next row (RS) K1, p1, k1, *p3tog, [k1, p1] twice, k1; rep from * to last 6 sts, end p3tog, k1, p1, k1—41 sts. Work 3 rows even. Rep last 4 rows once more—31 sts. **Next row (RS)** *K1, p1, k1, p3tog; rep from *, end k1—21 sts. Work 1 row even. **Next row (RS)** *K1, p3tog; rep from *, end k1—11 sts. **Next row** P1, [p2tog] 5 times—6 sts.

Top tab

Cont in St st on 6 sts for 4 rows. Cut yarn. Pull tight to gather and fasten securely. Sew back seam of top tab and hat.

SCARF

Bottom border

Note: Border is worked horizontally. Cast on 19 sts. **Row 1 (WS)** K3, *p2, k2; rep from * to end. **Row 2** *P2, k2; rep from *, end p3. Mark end of last row for top edge of border. Rep rows 1 and 2 for rib pat until piece measures 8"/20.5cm from beg, end with row 2. Bind off in rib pat. With RS of border facing, pick up and k 22 sts evenly spaced along top edge. **Row 1 (WS)** Sl 1 purlwise, *p1, k1; rep from *, end p1. **Row 2** Sl 1 knitwise, *k1, p1; rep from *, end k1. Rep last 2 rows for seed and sl st pat until piece measures 61"/155cm from beg, end with row 2. Bind off in pat.

Top border

Note: Border is worked horizontally. Cast on 19 sts. **Row 1 (WS)** *K2, p2; rep from *, end k3. **Row 2** P3, *k2, p2; rep from * to end. Mark beg of last row for top edge of border. Rep rows 1 and 2 for rib pat until piece measures 8"/20.5cm from beg, end with row 2. Bind off in rib pat.

FINISHING

Sew top edge of top border to edge of scarf. Block scarf lightly to measurements.

tea cozy hat

(Continued from page 74)

Beg chart

Crown shaping

Next row (RS) K1, k2tog, k41, ssk, place marker (pm), k2tog, k 41, ssk, k1. **Next row** P1, p2tog tbl, p39, p2tog, p2tog tbl, p39, p2tog, p1. **Next row** K1, k2tog, k37, ssk, k2tog, k37, ssk, k1. **Next row** P1, p2tog tbl, p35, p2tog, p2tog tbl, p35, p2tog, p1. In same way, cont to dec 4 sts every row until 8 sts rem. Cut yarn, thread through 8 sts, tighten and fasten securely. Sew center back seam. Fold lower edge to RS at turning ridge. Using MC and CC, make a tassel 3½"/9cm long and sew to top of hat.

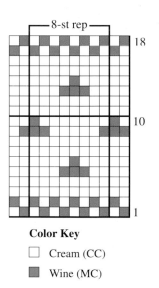

Color Key

☐ Cream (CC)

■ Wine (MC)

outerwear set

(Continued from page 76)

SEED STITCH

Row 1 K1, *p1, k1; rep from * to end.

Row 2 Knit the p sts and purl the k sts. Rep row 2 for seed st.

STRIPE PATTERN

Working in garter st, work as foll: 12 rows A, 6 rows MC, 6 rows B, 4 rows C, 8 rows MC, 6 rows D, 4 rows B), 8 rows E, 2 rows F, 6 rows A, 20 rows MC, 4 rows B, 4 rows MC, 6 rows C and 12 rows MC. Rep these 108 rows for stripe pat.

HAT

With larger needles and MC, cast on 59 sts. Work in k1, p1 rib for 4 rows, end with a WS row.

Beg chart

Row 1 (RS) Work in St st, beg with row 1, work 59 sts of chart through row 16. Change to MC to end of hat.

Crown shaping

Next row (RS) K1, [k2tog, k4] 9 times, end k2tog, k2—49 sts. P 1 row. **Next row (RS)** K1, [k2tog, k3] 9 times, end k2tog, k1—39 sts. P 1 row. **Next row (RS)** K1, [k2tog, k2] 9 times, end k2tog—29 sts. **Next row (WS)** [P2tog] 14 times, end p1—15 sts. **Next row** K1, [k2tog] 7 times—8 sts. Cut yarn. Pull tight to gather, fasten securely. Sew back seam.

Earflaps

With larger needles, RS facing and MC, pick up and k13 sts beg 6 sts from back seam. Work even in seed st for one row. Cont in seed st, dec 1 st at beg of every row 12 times. Bind off last st. Cut yarn, leave a 20"/51cm tail.

FINISHING

Embroidery

On front of hat, work as foll: with B, work a row of cross-stitches along left edge of diagonal motif, then a row of blanket stitches along right edge as shown. With D, work a row of running stitches across top edge of motif. On back of hat, work as foll: with D, work a row of blanket stitches along back seam from top edge of rib band to top edge of stripe motif. On right earflap, work as foll: with C, work over-cast stitches along back edge of flap leaving an 20"/51cm tail. With E, work over-cast stitches along front edge of flap leaving an 20"/51cm tail. On left earflap, work as for right flap, reversing colors.

Ties

Braid each group of tails for 12"/30.5cm. Make two 3½"/9cm tassels using MC, B, C, D and E. Sew tassels to ends of ties. Trim bottom edges.

SCARF

With larger needles and A, cast on 2 sts. Work in garter st and stripe pat, inc 1 st each side every other row 16 times—34 sts. **Next (inc) row (RS)** Inc 1 st, work to last 2 sts, end k2tog. Work one row even. Rep last 2 rows until 266 rows have been completed from beg. **Next row (RS)** Dec 1 st each side of this row, then every other row 15 times more. Bind off rem 2 sts.

FINISHING

Block lightly to measurements.

FINGERLESS MITTENS (make 2)

Beg at hand opening, with larger needles and MC, cast on 21 sts. Work in k1, p1 rib for 3 rows, inc 1 st at end of last row RS row—22 sts. **Row 1 (RS)** K11, join 2nd ball of MC and cast on 8 sts for thumb opening. Using spare needle or dpn, work back and forth in k1, p1 rib on these 8 sts for 3 rows. Drop 2nd yarn, with first ball of yarn k8 thumb opening sts, then k11 rem sts on LH needle—30 sts. **Row 2 and all WS rows through row 58** Purl. **Row 3** Knit.

Thumb shaping

Row 5 K10, k2tog, k6, k2tog, k10—28 sts. **Row 7** K9, k2tog, k6, k2tog, k9—26 sts. **Row 9** K8, k2tog, k6, k2tog, k8—24 sts. **Row 11** K7, k2tog, k6, k2tog, k7—22 sts. **Row 13** K6, k2tog, k6, k2tog, k6—20 sts. **Rows 15, 17 and 19** Knit.

Arm shaping

Row 21 K7, M1, k6, M1, k7—22 sts. **Rows 23, 25, 27, 29, 31** Knit. **Row 33** K8, M1, k6, M1, k8—24 sts. **Rows 35, 37 and 39** Knit. **Row 41** K9, M1, k6, M1, k9—26 sts. **Rows 43, 45 and 47** Knit. **Row 49** K10, M1, k6, M1, k10—28 sts. **Rows 51, 53 and 55** Knit. **Row 57** K11, M1, k6, M1, k11—30 sts.

Elbow patch

Row 59 (RS) With E, cast on 2 sts, then k first 2 sts; with MC, k26, k2tog. **Row 60** With MC, bind off first 2 sts, p22; with E, p6, then cast on 2 sts. Drop E. **Row 61** With A, cast on 1 st, k9; with MC, k19, k2tog. **Row 62** With MC, p20, with A, p10. Drop A. **Row 63** With F, cast on 1 st, k11; with MC, k17, k2tog. **Row 64** With MC, p18; with F, p12. Drop F. **Row 65** With D, cast on 1 st, k13; with MC, k15, k2tog. **Row 66** With MC, p16; with D, p14. Drop D. **Row 67** With C, k14; with MC, k16. **Row 68** With MC, p16; with C, p14. Drop C. **Row 69** With B, k2tog, k11; with MC, k17, inc 1 st. **Row 70** With MC, p18; with B, p12. Drop B. **Row 71** With E, k2tog, k9; with MC k19, inc 1 st. **Row 72** With MC, p20; with E, p10. Drop E. **Row 73** With A, k2tog, k7; with MC, k21, inc 1 st. **Row 74** With MC, cast on 2 sts, p24; with A, p4; with MC, k2—32 sts. Drop A. Work with MC only. **Row 75** Bind off first 2 sts, k to end—30 sts. **Row 76** Purl. **Row 77** Knit. **Row 78** Purl, inc 1 st—31 sts. Cont in k1, p1 rib for 4 rows. Bind off loosely in rib.

CARGO POCKET (make 2)

With smaller needles and B, cast on 6 sts. **Rows 1 and 3** (WS) Purl **Row 2 (RS)** Knit. **Row 4** Cast on 2 sts, k6, cast on 2 sts—10 sts. **Row 5** Knit (for turning ridge). **Rows 6, 8, 10 and 12** P2, [k2,p2] twice. **Rows 7, 9, 11 and 13** K2, [p2, k2] twice. Bind off.

Pocket flap

With smaller needles and B, cast on 6 sts. **Row 1 (WS)** Purl. **Row 2** Inc 1 st, k6, inc 1 st—8 sts. **Row 3 (buttonhole row)** P4, M1, p4—9 sts. **Row 4** Knit. **Row 5** Purl. Bind off knitwise.

FINISHING

Block lightly to measurements. Sew side seam of thumb opening.

Cargo pocket

Sew cast-on edges of row 4 to side edges of beg cast-on. Sew back edges of pocket 1¾"/4.5cm from hand opening. Sew top edge of flap ½"/1.5cm above top edge of pocket. Sew on button. Sew side and elbow patch seams. With B, work a row of blanket stitches around each elbow patch.

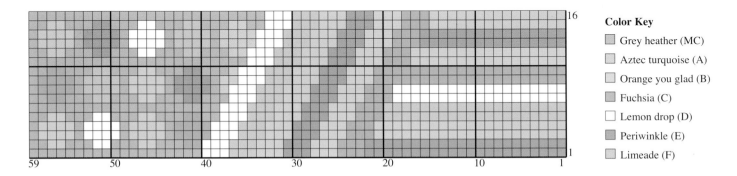

Color Key

- Grey heather (MC)
- Aztec turquoise (A)
- Orange you glad (B)
- Fuchsia (C)
- Lemon drop (D)
- Periwinkle (E)
- Limeade (F)

pompom hat

(Continued from page 78)

Next rnd *K2tog, rep from *, end k1—18 sts. K 3 rnds. **Next rnd** *k2tog; rep from * around—9 sts. K 1 rnd. Cut yarn, leaving an end. Thread yarn through sts on needle and pull tog tightly. Make 5 extra-thick 2½"/6.5cm pompoms. Sew one on center top of hat and other 4 around center.

sherpa hat and scarf

(Continued from page 80)

HAT

With larger needles, cast on 14 sts. Knit 6 rows. **Next (inc) row** K to last st, M1, k1. Work 1 row even. Rep last 2 rows 10 times more—25 sts. Work 2 rows even. **Next (dec) row** K to last 2 sts, k2tog tbl. K 3 rows even. Rep last 4 rows 10 times more—14 sts. **Next (inc) row** K to last st, M1, k1. K 3 rows even. Rep last 4 rows 10 times more—25 sts. **Next (dec) row** K to last 2 sts, k2tog tbl. K 1 row even. Rep last 2 rows 10 times more—14 sts. Work 6 rows even. Bind off. Sew seam.

Crown

With dpn, pick up 72 sts from inside of top of piece, 4 sts down from edge. Join and k 5 rnds. **Next (dec) rnd** *K7, p2tog; rep from * to end—64 sts. Work 2 rnds even. **Next (dec) rnd** *K6, p2tog; rep from * to end—56 sts. Work 1 rnd even. Cont in this way to dec 8 sts every other rnd, working 1 less st between dec every dec rnd, until there are 8 sts. Cut yarn and draw through rem sts.

SCARF

With larger needles, cast on 2 sts. **Row 1** K1, M1, k1. K 3 rows even. Cont to inc 1 st in last st every other row 17 times more—20 sts. Work even for 24 rows. Change to smaller needles and work 12 rows twisted rib. Change to larger needles and work even in garter st for 92 rows. Change to smaller needles and work 12 rows twisted rib. Change to larger needles and work even for 24 rows. **Next (dec) row** K to last 2 sts, k2tog tbl. Work 1 row even. Cont to dec 1 st at end of every other row 17 times more—2 sts. Cut yarn and draw through rem sts.

Casing

With smaller needles, pick up 18 sts from beg of one side of twisted rib. Work 10 rows twisted rib. Bind off. Sew bound-off edge to other side of twisted rib.

cable scarf

(Continued from page 82)

FINISHING

Block lightly.

Fringe

Cut 16"/40.5cm strands of A and B. Using a double strand for each, use hook to knot fringe foll color sequence and incorporating tails into fringe. Trim fringe evenly.

snowflake hat

(Continued from page 84)

under joining marker for center back.

Beg chart

Rnd 1 Work 16-st rep 7 times. Work through chart rnd 28. With MC, k2 rnds. **Next rnd** *K1C, k3MC; rep from *. **With MC, p 1 rnd, then k 1 rnd.** **Dec rnd 1** With MC, *k2, k2tog; rep from * — 84 sts. **Next rnd** *K2MC, k1C; rep from *. Rep between **'s once. **Dec rnd 2** With MC, *k1, k2tog; rep from * — 56 sts. **Next rnd** *K1C, k1MC; rep from *. Rep between **'s once. Cont with MC only. **Dec rnd 3** *K2tog; rep from * — 28 sts. K 3 rnds. **Dec rnd 4** *K2tog; rep from * — 14 sts. K 1 rnd. **Dec rnd 5** [K2tog] 7 times — 7 sts. **Dec rnd 6** [Sl 1, k2tog, psso] twice, k1. Fasten off.

Earflaps

(Note: Work back and forth in rows on dpn.) **Right earflap** With RS facing, dpn and A, beg 12 sts to right of center back and pick up and k20 sts. K 1 row. Work 6 rows in garter check pat. **Next row (RS)** K2A, ssk, cont pat row 3 to last 4 sts, k2tog, k2A. In same way, dec 1 st each side every other row 5 times more — 8 sts. With A, k2 rows. Bind off.

Left earflap Beg 12 sts to left of center back marker and work as for right earflap.

FINISHING

With MC, make pompom. Attach to top of hat.

Ties With hook, join A to center of right earflap. Ch 40.

Work 1 sc in 2nd ch from hook and in each ch across.

Sl st to flap. Fasten off. Rep for 2nd flap. Block hat.

Stitch Key

⊞ K on RS, p on WS with cream (MC)

⊟ P on RS, k on WS with cream (MC)

☐ Burgundy (B)

⊡ Dark camel (C)

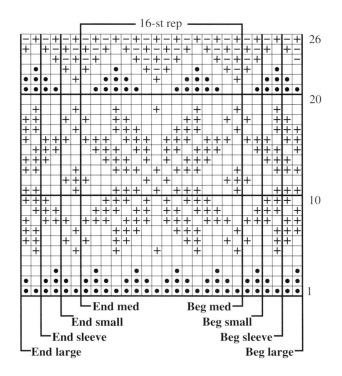

fair isle hat and scarf

(Continued from page 88)

Beg chart 1

Row 1 (RS) Beg with st 1 of chart, work to st 7, then work sts 2-7 (6 st rep) 9 times. Cont in chart as established through row 20.

With MC, cont in St st for 2 rows.

Crown shaping

Next row (RS) K1, [k2tog, k4] 5 times—51 sts. P 1 row. **Next row (RS)** K1, [k2tog, k3] 5 times—41 sts. P 1 row. **Next row (RS)** K1, [k2tog, k2] 5 times—31 sts. P 1 row. **Next row (RS)** K1, [k2tog, k1] 5 times—21 sts. **Next row (WS)** P1, [p2tog] 5 times—11 sts. Cut yarn. Pull through sts and fasten securely. Sew back seam, reversing seam for lower 3"/7.6cm for cuff.

FINISHING

With MC, make a 3"/7.5cm pompom. Sew to top of hat.

SCARF

With MC, cast on 22 sts. Work in garter st for 7 rows, inc 3 sts evenly across last WS row—25 sts. Work in St st for 4 rows.

Beg chart 1

Row 1 (RS) Beg with st 1, work to st 7, then work sts 2-7 (6 st rep) 3 times. Cont in chart as established through row 20. With MC, cont in St st until piece measures 58"/147.5cm from beg, end with a WS.

Beg chart 2

Row 1 (RS) Beg with st 1 of chart and work to st 7, then work sts 2-7 (6 st rep) 3 times. Cont in chart as established through row 20. With MC cont in St st for 6 rows, dec 3 sts across last WS row—22 sts. Work in garter st for 6 rows. Bind off knitwise.

FINISHING

Block lightly to measurements.

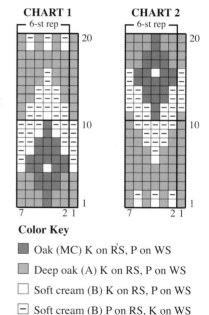

CHART 1 **CHART 2**

Color Key

■ Oak (MC) K on RS, P on WS

▨ Deep oak (A) K on RS, P on WS

□ Soft cream (B) K on RS, P on WS

⊟ Soft cream (B) P on RS, K on WS

fair isle hat

(Continued from page 90)

dec rnd k3 as foll: *ssk, k1, pm, k1, k2tog, k7; rep from *, end k4—88 sts. **Next rnd** With D, knit. **Next rnd** With C, work to 3 sts before marker, ssk, k2, k2tog, k5; rep from * around—72 sts. Rep last 2 rnds twice—40 sts. **Next (dec) rnd** Work to 3 sts between decs, *sl 2 knitwise, k1, psso, k2; rep from * around—24 sts. **Next rnd** With A, knit. **Next (dec) rnd** With A, *k1, k2tog; rep from * around—16 sts. **Next rnd** With A, knit. **Next (dec) rnd** *K2tog; rep from * around—8 sts. Cut yarn leaving 6"/15.5cm tail and thread through rem sts. Pull tog tightly and secure end.

Earflaps

With hat upside down, RS and center back facing, beg in 18th st to the left of center back, with A, pick up and k 21 sts. **Row 1 (WS)** With A knit. Cont to work back and forth in garter st as foll: K 4 rows A, 4 rows C. **Next row (RS)** *Sl 1, k1 D; rep from *, end sl 1. **Next row** *Sl, bring yarn to back, k1, bring yarn to front; rep from *, end sl. **Next row (RS)** *K1 C, sl 1; rep from *, end k1 C. K 2 rows with B. K 4 rows with A. **Eyelet dec row** With C, k2, k2tog, yo, ssk, k to last 6 sts, k2tog, yo, ssk, k2—19 sts. **Next row** With C, knit. Rep last 2 rows twice—15 sts. **Next 6 rows** With A, rep eyelet dec row every RS row 3 times—9 sts. **Next row** A, k1, k2tog, yo, sl 2 knitwise, k1, psso, yo, ssk, k1—7 sts. **Next row** Knit. **Last row** Ssk, sl 1, k2tog, psso, bind off, k2tog, bind off last st.

Work 2nd earflap opposite first.

FINISHING

With RS facing and crochet hook, beg at center back lower edge of hat, work sc evenly all along lower edge, alternating 1 st A and 1 st C, and substituting D for C along curved edges of each flap.

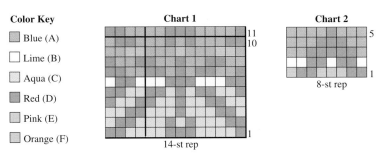

Color Key

- ☐ Blue (A)
- ☐ Lime (B)
- ☐ Aqua (C)
- ☐ Red (D)
- ☐ Pink (E)
- ☐ Orange (F)

Chart 1

14-st rep

Chart 2

8-st rep

beaded scarf

(Continued from page 92)

FEATHERED FAGGOT (FF) (over 4 sts)

Row 1 K1, yo, p2tog, k1. Rep row 1 for FF.

FRINGE

1 abacus 4mm jet	6 shiny black	thread through glass fired bead
6 shiny black Japanese seed beads	1 abacus	6 matte black
1 glass fired polished bead 4mm jet	1 glass teardrop bead 6x4mm jet	thread through glass fired bead
6 matte black seed	turn then thread through abacus	6 shiny black
1 glass fired polished bead	6 shiny black	thread through abacus

SCARF

Using long tail method, cast on 1 st with waxed beading thread around thumb (12yd/11.5m long, doubled length will give you enough to complete fringe and cont along one side of scarf. Add another length of waxed beading thread at beg of next row for the other side), make one fringe and pull tight, *cast on 1 st with yarn then bead next fringe and finish cast-on; rep from * (beaded fringe is added every other st) until there are 30 fringe—60 sts in total. Work in pat as foll:

Row 1 (RS) Work 6 sts seed st, 4 FF, 2 sts seed st, 4 FF, 4 sts seed st, 8 FF, 4 sts seed st, 8 FF, 4 sts seed st, 4 FF, 2 sts seed st, 4 FF, 6 sts seed st

Row 2 Beg 2nd bead thread with leftover from cast-on fringe, bead 1 abacus and 1 shiny black seed, p1 with bead thread and yarn held tog, drop bead thread and cont in pat as established with yarn only.

Row 3 Bead 1 abacus, 1 matte black and cont same as row 1.

Row 4 Bead 1 abacus, 1 matte black and cont same as row 2.

Rep last 2 rows, alternate shiny and matte black beads, until piece measures 36"/91.5cm from beg.

Bind off, attaching bead fringe same as on cast-on edge.

FINISHING

Block lightly to measurements.

ribbed hat and scarf set

(Continued from page 96)

Shape top

Next row (RS) [K2tog, k1, p2, k3, p2] 7 times—63 sts. Work 3 rows even. **Next row** [K2, p2, k2tog, k1, p2] 7 times—56 sts. Work 3 rows even. **Next row** [K2, p2tog, k2, p2] 7 times—49 sts. Work 1 row even. **Next row** [K2, p1, k2, p2tog] 7 times—42 sts. Work 1 row even. **Next row** [K2tog, p1, k2, p1] 7 times—35 sts. Work 1 row even. **Next row** [K1, p1, k2tog, p1] 7 times—28 sts. **Next row** [P2tog, p2] 7 times—21 sts. **Next row** [K1, k2tog] 7 times—14 sts. **Next row** [P2tog] 7 times—7 sts. **Next row** [K2tog] twice, k3tog—3 sts. Cut yarn and draw through rem sts.

FINISHING

Block very lightly. Sew back seam, reversing seam at lower edge for turnback.

SCARF

Cast on 33 sts. K 3 rows. **Next row (RS)** K3, [p2, k3] 6 times. **Next row** K3, rib to last 3 sts, k3. Rep last 2 rows until piece measures 51"/129.5cm, end with a RS row. K 3 rows. Bind off.

FINISHING

Block very lightly.

1. After sts are cast on one needle, divide them evenly over three needles. Place a marker for end of the rnd and begin knitting in rib, making sure the sts are not twisted.

2. When decreasing for top shaping, if you come to a dec with the two sts on separate needles, place both sts on the same needle to make it easier to knit them together.

3. After all decreases have been worked (3 sts remaining), place them on one needle. Cut the yarn, thread it through a sewing needle and draw it through the sts on the knitting needle to secure them.

4. If you have worked the hat back and forth on two needles, when sewing the back seam, reverse the seam at the lower edge, as shown, so it will not show when the cuff is turned to the right side.

argyle scarf and socks

(Continued from page 98)

• One pair each sizes 2 and 3 (2.75 and 3mm) needles OR SIZE TO OBTAIN GAUGE

• Bobbins

• St markers

GAUGE

Scarf

26 sts and 32 rows = 4"/10cm over St st foll chart using size 4 (3.5mm) needles.

Socks

28 sts and 36 rows/rnds = 4"/10cm over St st foll chart using size 3 (3mm) dpn.

TAKE TIME TO CHECK GAUGE.

Chart #1

13

1

30-st rep

Notes:1) All single color cross lines on argyle pat chart should be worked in duplicate st after pieces are completed. 2) Wind A, B and C onto bobbins and work each separate block of color with a separate bobbin. Twist yarns tog at each color change to avoid holes in work. Do not carry yarn across back of work.

SCARF

With size 4 (3.5mm) needles and A, cast on 69 sts. **Row 1** Knit. **Row 2** K1 (selvage st), p to last st, k1 (selvage st). Rep last 2 rows 5 times more (there are 12 rows in A).

Beg chart 1

Row 1 (RS) With A, k4, work 30-st rep of row 1 of chart 1 twice, work last st of chart, with A, k4. Cont to foll chart 1 in this way through row 13. With A, work in St st for 11 rows, dec 1 st at center on last WS row—68 sts.

Beg chart 2

Row 1 (RS) With A, k4, work 60 sts of row 1 of chart 2, with A, k4. Cont to foll chart in this way working 58-row rep a total of 7 times, then work rows 1-29 once more. With A, p1 row inc 1 st at center—69 sts. Cont in St st with A only for 11 rows more. Work 1 rep of chart 1 as before. Then work 12 rows in St st with A only. Bind off.

FINISHING

Work all cross lines in duplicate st foll chart. Block to measurements. Taking in a selvage of ½"/1.5cm from scarf edges and 2 sts at outer edge of scarf, whip st knitted scarf to fabric backing scarf.

Note: If necessary, cut scarf with pinking shears to fit knitted piece and cut in half at center and re-stitch to accurately fit length of scarf.

SOCKS

Beg at cuff edge with size 2 (2.75mm) straight needles and A, cast on 62 sts. **Row 1 (RS)** K1 (selvage st), *k2, p2; rep from *, end k1 (selvage st). Work in k2, p2 rib as established for 2"/5cm. Change to size 3 (3mm) straight needles.

Beg Chart 2

Row 1 (RS) K1, (selvage st), work 60 sts of row 1 of chart 2, k1 (selvage st). Cont to work in this way through row 58 of chart, dec 1 selvage st each side on last WS row —60 sts.

Heel

On next row, sl first 15 sts onto one size 3 (3.25mm) dpn and last 15 sts of same row onto other end of same needle, divide rem 30 sts onto 2 needles to be worked later for instep. Work on 30 sts for heel only in A as foll: **Row 1 (RS)** *Wyib, sl 1 purlwise, k1; rep from * to end. **Row 2** Sl 1 purlwise, p to end. Rep these 2 rows until heel measures 2½"/6.5cm. Pm at center of heel (in between 15 sts each side) on last WS row.

Turn heel

Row 1 (RS) K to 2 sts after center marker, ssk, k1, turn. **Row 2** Sl 1, p to 2 sts after center marker, p2tog, p1, turn. **Row 3** Sl 1, k to 3 sts after center marker, ssk, k1, turn. **Row 4** Sl 1, p to 3 sts after center marker, p2tog, p1, turn. Cont to work in this way, working to 1 more st after marker first on RS then on WS row until all sts are worked and 18 sts rem in heel. K 1 row on RS. Sl first 9 sts to spare needle, second 9 sts to needle 1. With A, and cont on end of needle 1, pick up and k 18 sts along side (rows) of heel, pm; with needle 2, k 30 instep sts; pm; with needle 3, pick up and k 18 sts along side (rows) of heel, sl 9 sts from beg onto end of needle 3. Cut yarn and rejoin to beg working in rnds at center of heel—84 sts. Pm at this point and work in rnds with A only.

Shape instep

Rnd 1 Knit. **Rnd 2** K to 3 sts before first marker, k2tog, k1, k to 3rd marker, k1, ssk, k to end. Rep last 2 rnds 11 times more—60 sts. Work even in rnds of St st until foot measures 8½"/21.5cm from back of heel or 2"/5cm less than desired length of foot.

Shape toe

Rnd 1 Needle 1 K to last 3 sts, k2tog, k1; Needle 2 K1, ssk, k to last 3 sts, k2tog, k1; Needle 3 K1, ssk, k to end. **Rnd 2** Knit. Rep last 2 rnds 10 times more—16 sts. Divide sts onto 2 needles and weave toe tog using Kitchener st.

FINISHING

Work all cross lines in duplicate st foll chart. Block to measurements. Sew back seam of cuff and leg.

Chart #2

← 60 st rep →

Color Key
⊠ Black (A)   ☐ White (B)   ⊡ Turquoise (C)

folk hat

(Continued from page 100)

- Size 2 (2.5mm) circular needle, 16"/40cm long OR SIZE TO OBTAIN GAUGE

- One set size 2 (2.5mm) dpn

- St marker

GAUGE

32 sts and 30 rows = 4"10cm over chart pats using size 2 (2.5mm) needles.

TAKE TIME TO CHECK GAUGE.

Note: When there are too few sts to fit on circular needle, switch to dpn.

HAT

With circular needle and A, cast on 168 sts. Join and pm. K 1 rnd, p 1 rnd.

Beg charts

Rnds 3-6 Work 8-st rep of chart I 21 times..

Rnds 7-10 With A, knit. Rnds 11-40 Work 42-st rep of chart II 4 times. Dec rnd 41 [K4 C, k4 B, k1 C, k2tog C, k2 C, k3 B, k7 C, k3 B, k1 C, k2tog C, k2 C, k4 B, k4 C, k3 B] 4 times—160 sts. Rnds 42-44 With C, knit. Dec rnd 45 With C, k4, *k2tog, k6; rep from *, end k2—140 sts. Rnds 46-48 With A, knit. Dec rnd 49 Work rnd 1 of chart III—120 sts. Rnds 50-58 Work rnds 2-10 of chart III. Dec rnd 59 With A, *k3, k2tog; rep from * to end—96 sts. Rnd 60 With A, knit. Rnds 61-65 Work 6-st rep of chart IV 16 times. Dec rnd 66 With C, k1, *k2tog, k2; rep from *, end k1—72 sts. Rnds 67 and 68 With C, knit. Rnds 69-75 Work 12-st rep of chart V 6 times. Dec rnd 76 With A, k1, *k2tog, k2; rep from *, end k1—54 sts. Rnds 77 and 78 With A, knit. *K1, k2tog; rep from * to end — 36 sts. Rnd 79 *K1, K2tog; rep from * to end — 36 sts. Rnd 80 Knit. Rnd 81 *K1, k2tog; rep from * to end—24 sts. Rnd 82 Knit. Dec rnd 83 *K2tog; rep from * around—12 sts. Cut yarn and pull through rem sts.

Color Key (K on RS, p on WS)

- Black (A)
- Cream (B)
- Brown Tweed (C)
- Sand (D)
- K2tog with Black (A)
- Ssk or K2tog matching color

Color Key (K on WS)

- Black (A)
- Cream (B)
- Brown Tweed (C)
- Sand (D)

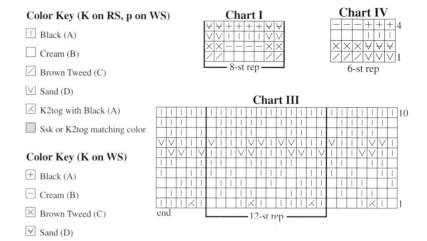

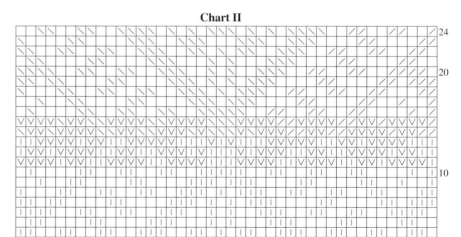

EARFLAP

(make 2)

With dpn and A, cast on 70 sts.

Beg chart VI

Row 1 (RS) Work sts 1-35, then work sts 35-1. Cont as established through row 4. **Dec row 5 (RS)** K33, ssk, with 3rd needle, k2tog, work to end—34 sts on each needle. Cont foll chart, work 2 decs at center every row through row 26—13 sts on each needle. Graft rem sts tog.

FINISHING

Sew earflaps to sides of cap halfway between center front and back.

Pompoms

With A, B, C and D, make 2 each, 2"/5cm, 1½"/4cm and 1"/2.5cm pompoms. Attach to a 5"/12.5cm braid of A and C.

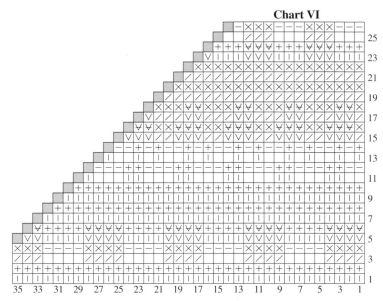

Chart VI

Color Key (K on RS, p on WS)

- Black (A)
- Cream (B)
- Brown Tweed (C)
- Sand (D)
- K2tog with Black (A)
- Ssk or K2tog matching color

Color Key (K on WS)

- Black (A)
- Cream (B)
- Brown Tweed (C)
- Sand (D)

andes cap

(Continued from page 100)

For hat only

- Size 2 (2.5mm) circular needle, 16"/40cm long OR SIZE TO OBTAIN GAUGE

- One set size 2 (2.5mm) dpn

For scarf only

- One pair each sizes 2 and 3 (2.5 and 3mm) needles OR SIZE TO OBTAIN GAUGE

- St holder

GAUGE

32 sts and 30 rows = 4"10cm over chart pats using size 2 (2.5mm) needles.

TAKE TIME TO CHECK GAUGE.

HAT

Note: When there are too few sts to fit on circular needle, switch to dpn.

With circular needle and D, cast on 160 sts. Join and pm. **Rnd 1** With B, [k1 tbl, p1] 3 times, k1 tbl, *yo, k1, yo, [k1 tbl, p1] 7 times, k1 tbl; rep from *, end yo, k1, yo, [k1 tbl, p1] 4 times. **Rnd 2** [K1 tbl, p1] 3 times, k1 tbl, *k1, p1, p1, [k1 tbl, p1] 7 times, k1 tbl; rep from *, end last rep [k1 tbl, p1] 4 times. **Rnd 3** With C, [k1 tbl, p1] 3 times, k1 tbl, *yo, k3, yo, [k1 tbl, p1] 7 times, k1 tbl; rep from *, end yo, k3, yo, [k1 tbl, p1] 4 times. **Rnd 4** [K1 tbl, p1] 3 times, k1 tbl, *k1, p3, k1, [k1 tbl, p1] 7 times, k1 tbl; rep from *, end last rep [k1 tbl, p1] 4 times. **Rnd 5** With D, [k1 tbl, p1] 3 times, k1 tbl, *yo, k5, yo, [k1 tbl, p1] 7 times, k1 tbl; rep from *, end yo, k5, yo, [k1 tbl, p1] 4 times. **Rnd 6** [K1 tbl, p1] 3 times, k1 tbl, *k1, p5, k1, [k1 tbl, p1] 7 times, k1 tbl; rep from *, end last rep [k1 tbl, p1] 4 times. **Rnd 7** [K1 tbl, p1] 3 times, k1 tbl, *yo, k7, yo, [k1 tbl, p1] 7 times, k1 tbl; rep from *, end yo, k7, yo, [k1 tbl, p1] 4 times—240 sts. **Rnd 8** [K1 tbl, p1] 3 times, k1 tbl, *k1, p7, k1, [k1 tbl, p1] 7 times, k1 tbl; rep from *, end last rep [k1 tbl, p1] 4 times. **Dec rnd 9** [Ssk] 3 times, k1, *k9, [ssk] 3 times, SK2P, [k2tog] 3 times; rep from *, end k8, SK2P, [k2tog] 3 times—160 sts. **Rnds 10-18** Rep rnds 1-9. **Rnd 19** With D, knit. **Rnd 20** With E, knit. **Rnds 21-23** With F, knit. **Rnd 24** With F, k1, *with G MB, k3 F; rep from *, using different colors for each bobble, end k2. K 1 rnd F, 1 rnd E, 1 rnd C, 2 rnds B, 1 rnd G.

Beg charts

Work 4 rnds chart I, 11 rnds chart II, 4 rnds chart III, 5 rnds chart IV, 4 rnds chart V, 4 rnds chart VI, 3 rnds chart VII, 6 rnds chart VIII, 4 rnds chart IX—54 sts. **Next rnd** *K1, k2tog; rep from * to end—36 sts. K 1 rnd. **Next rnd** *K2tog; rep from * around—18 sts. K 1 rnd. **Next rnd** *K2tog; rep from * around—9 sts. Cut yarn leaving and draw through rem sts.

SCARF

Lace pattern (over 43 sts)

Row 1 (RS) K3, *yo, k2, ssk, k2tog, k2, yo, k1; rep from *, end yo, k2, ssk. **Rows 2 and 4** Purl. **Row 3** K2, *yo, k2, ssk, k2tog, k2, yo, k1; rep from *, end yo, k2, ssk, k1. Rep rows 1-4 for lace pat.

Rib Pattern

Color Key

☐ Lt green (A)
☒ Copper tweed (B)
⊟ Red tweed (C)
▪ Purple (D)
⊠ Lt olive green (E)
⊞ Caramel (F)
✦ Blue (G)
△ Yellow tweed (H)
○ Rose tweed (I)
Ι Plum tweed (J)
╱ K2tog
● MB in desired color

Chart I

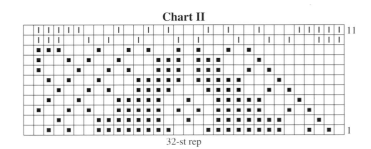

4-st rep

Chart V

18-st rep

Chart VI

12-st rep

Chart II

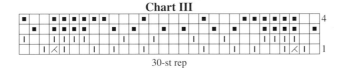

32-st rep

Chart III

30-st rep

Chart IV

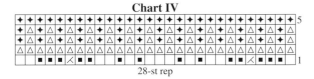

28-st rep

Chart VII

10-st rep

Chart VIII

8-st rep

Chart IX

6-st rep

Row 1 (RS) K2, *p3, k3; rep from *, end p3, k2. **Row 2** K the knit sts and p the purl sts. Rep row 2

for rib pat.

With larger needles and C, cast on 49 sts. **Row 1 (RS)** With E, k1, *yo, [k1tbl, p1] 7 times, k1 tbl,

yo, k1; rep from * to end—55 sts. **Row 2** K1, *p1, [p1 tbl, k1] 7 times, p1 tbl, p1, k1; rep from * to

end. **Row 3** With D, k2, *yo, [k1 tbl, p1] 7 times, k1 tbl, yo, k3; rep from *, end last rep yo, k2—61

sts. **Row 4** K2, *p1, [p1 tbl, k1] 7 times, p1 tbl, p1, k3; rep from *, end last rep p1, k2. **Row 5** With

F, k3, *yo, [k1 tbl, p1] 7 times, k1 tbl, yo, k5; rep from *, end last rep yo, k3—67 sts. **Row 6** K3, *p1,

[p1 tbl, k1] 7 times, p1 tbl, p1, k5; rep from *, end last rep p1, k3. **Row 7** K4, *yo, [k1 tbl, p1] 7 times,

k1 tbl, yo, k7; rep from *, end last rep yo, k4—73 sts. **Row 8** K4, *p1, [p1 tbl, k1] 7 times, p1 tbl, p1,

k7; rep from *, end last rep p1, k4. **Row 9** K5, *[ssk] 3 times, SK2P, [k2tog] 3 times, k9; rep from *,

end k5—49 sts. **Row 10** With C, purl. Rep rows 1-10 once more. Change to smaller needles.

Beg chart X

Next row (RS) With I, k3, work 43 sts chart X, k3 I. Cont in pat as established, working first and

last 3 sts in garter st, matching colors from chart, through row 88. Cont in lace pat as foll: 8 rows

A, 2 rows D, 6 rows A, 6 rows J, 2 rows E, 2 rows J, 2 rows A, dec 3 sts evenly on last WS row—

46 sts. Work in rib pat as foll: 8 rows A, 4 rows I, 2 rows G, 2 rows C, 4 rows B, 2 rows A, 2 rows

D, 6 rows A, 2 rows H, 4 rows G, 2 rows A, 8 rows D, 4 rows B, 2 rows C, 4 rows E, 2 rows I, 4

rows H, 2 rows A, 6 rows J, 2 rows E, 4 rows B, 4 rows G, 2 rows C, 4 rows I, 8 rows A, 4 rows

D, 2 rows E, 2 rows F, 4 rows D. Sl sts to a holder.

Work a 2nd piece in same way. Weave sts tog for center back.

POMPOMS

Make 4 large and 4 medium pompoms using various colors, leaving an

8"/20.5cm tail on large pompom and 4"/10cm tail on small pompom.

Secure end of tails to lower edges of scarf between scallops.

Color Key

☐ Lt green (A)

☒ Copper tweed (B)

— Red tweed (C)

■ Purple (D)

⊠ Lt olive green (E)

⊞ Caramel (F)

✦ Blue (G)

△ Yellow tweed (H)

○ Rose tweed (I)

▮ Plum tweed (J)

⧄ K2tog

⬤ MB in desired color

Chart X

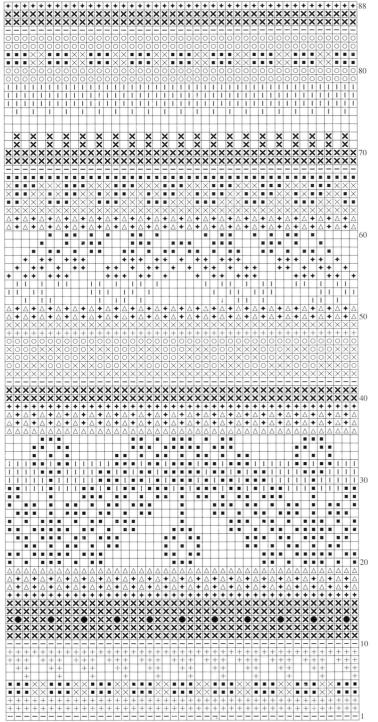

43 sts

nordic set

(Continued from page 104)

with A in St st. Bind off.

FINISHING

Block scarf to measurements. Fold in half lengthwise and sew side and lower edge seams.

HAT

Beg at lower edge with A, cast on 98 sts. Work in k1, p1 rib for 10 rows, then St st for 2 rows.

Beg chart 1

Row 1 (RS) K1 (selvage st), beg on row 41 of chart 1, work 24-st rep 4 times, k1 (selvage st). Cont to foll chart through row 56. With A, k 1 row. P next row, dec 6 sts evenly across—92 sts.

Beg chart 2

Row 1 (RS) K1 (selvage st), work 18-st rep of chart 2 five times, k1 (selvage st). Cont to foll chart 2 through row 12. **Row 13 (RS)** K1 (selvage st), *k4 sts of chart, k2tog, pm, k7 sts of chart, pm, k2tog, k3 sts of chart; rep from * 4 times more, k1 (selvage st)—82 sts. Work 1 row even. **Next row** K1, *k to 2 sts before first marker, k2tog, k to 2nd marker, k2tog; rep from * 4 times more, k to end—72 sts. Rep last 2 rows once more—62 sts. Cont with A only, dec 10 sts every other row twice more—42 sts. P 1 row. **Next row** [K2tog, k1] 14 times—28 sts. P 1 row. **Next row** [K2tog] 14 times. Cut yarn, leaving long end. Pull through rem sts, draw up tightly and secure. Sew back seam. Fold rib hem to WS and sew in place. Make a 3"/7.5cm pompom in colors A and B and attach to top of hat.

Chart #1 part 1

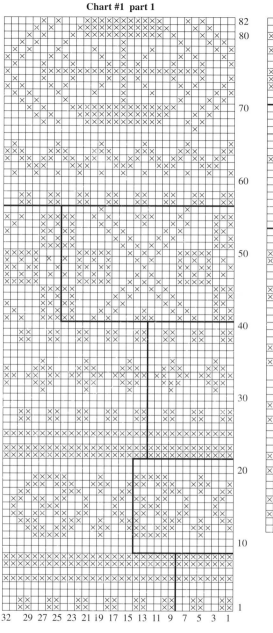

32 29 27 25 23 21 19 17 15 13 11 9 7 5 3 1

Chart #1 part 2

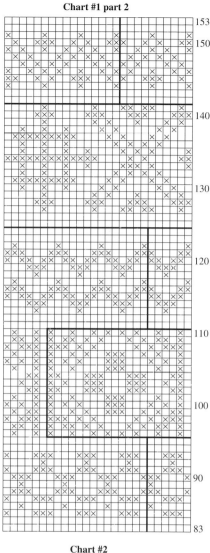

Chart #2

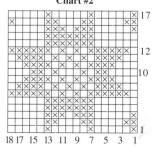

18 17 15 13 11 9 7 5 3 1

Color Key
☐ Black (A)
☒ Turquoise (B)

his-and-hers

argyle ties

(Continued from page 106)

same st back to LH needle (1 purl st wrapped), turn. **Next row** Work to last 4 sts, wrap st, turn. **Next row** Work to last 4 sts, wrap next st, turn. Cont in this way to work 2 less sts at end of every row, until 1 st rem. Cut yarn.

Lining of small point

With RS facing, join MC to beg of row and k to end, working the extra wrap tog with the wrapped st. Cont with MC only as foll: K next row on WS. Mark center st. **Next row (RS)** Bind off 10 sts, work to 1 st before center st, work double dec (sl 2, k1, pass 2 slipped st over k1), k to end. Bind off 10 sts at beg of next row, p to end. Cont to work double dec in center every knit row until there are 5 sts. Bind off.

Lining of large point

With RS facing, join MC and pick up 1 st in each cast-on st of large point — 59 sts. Cont with MC only as foll: P 1 row on WS. Mark center st. **Next row (RS)** Bind off 14 sts, work to 1 st before center st, work double dec, k to end. Bind off 14 sts at beg of next row, p to end. Cont to work double dec in center every knit row until there are 5 sts. Bind off.

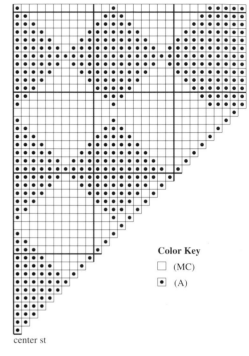

Color Key

☐ (MC)

⊡ (A)

center st

FINISHING

With MC, embroider a small "x" in center of CC diamonds. Steam lightly. Fold and pin tie ends over the top of the linings. Roll the purl ridges slightly to the underside of the points. Sew without catching the front of the tie. Sew the center seam without catching the front of the tie. Steam again.

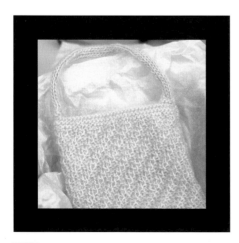

diagonal-stitch handbag

(Continued from page 108)

Strap

With RS facing and dpn, pick up 5 sts along bag edge, with center st on seam. Work I-cord as foll: **Next row (RS)** *K5, do not turn. Slide sts to beg of needle to work the next row from RS; rep from * until I-cord measures 14"/35.5cm. Graft stitches to other edge of bag.

Lining

Cut 2 rectangles, 8" x 8½"/20.5cm x 21.5cm. With right sides together, seam along sides and bottom ½"/1.5cm from edge. Trim seams, press them open. Press under 1"/2.5cm at open end, trim. Place lining in bag (wrong sides together) and stitch top of lining to bag edging.

men's cabled mittens

(Continued from page 110)

- St markers
- St holders

GAUGE

22 sts and 38 rows = 4"/10cm over seed st using size 3 (3.25mm) needles.

TAKE TIME TO CHECK GUAGE.

SEED STITCH

Rnd 1 *K1, p1; rep from *. **Rnd 2** P the k sts and k the p sts. Rep rnd 2 for seed st.

CABLE PATTERN (worked over 10 sts)

Rnds 1 and 3 Knit. **Rnd 2** K2, [sl 2 sts to cn and hold to front, k2, k2 from cn] twice. **Rnd 4** [Sl 2 sts to cn and hold to back, k2, k2 from cn] twice, k2. Rep rnds 1–4 for cable pat.

RIGHT MITTEN

Cast on 60 sts and divide sts evenly over 3 needles. Join, mark beg of rnd. Work in k2, p2 ribbing for 3½"/9cm. K next rnd, dec 4 sts evenly spaced—56 sts. **Next rnd** Work seed st over 9 sts, place marker (pm), work cable pat, beg with rnd 1, over 10 sts, pm, work seed st to end of rnd. Rep this rnd 3 times more.

Shape Thumb

Next Rnd Work seed st over 9 sts, sl marker, work rnd 1 of cable pat, sl marker, work seed st over 11 sts, pm, inc 1 in next st, work next st in seed st as established, inc 1 in next st, pm, work to end of rnd in seed st. Work 2 rnds in pats as established. **Next rnd** Work seed st over 9 sts, sl marker, work cable pat, sl marker, work seed st to next marker, inc 1 in next st, work seed st to 1 st before next marker, inc 1 in next st, sl marker, work to end of rnd in seed st. Rep last 3 rnds until there are 17 sts between thumb markers. **Next rnd** Work to first thumb marker, sl next 17 sts to a holder, cast on 3 sts, work to end—56 sts. Cont in pats as established until mitten measures approx 4½"/11.5cm above thumb.

Shape top

Next rnd Cont as established, dec 7 sts evenly spaced on seed st portion of mitten. Work 4 rnds even, then rep dec rnd having 1 less st between decs—42 sts. Work 3 rnds even, rep dec rnd—35 sts. Work 2 rnds even, rep dec rnd—28 sts. Work 1 rnd even. **Next rnd** Work cable as established, k2tog, p2tog over seed sts. Work 1 rnd even. **Next rnd** K2tog around (including cable sts). Break yarn and pull end through rem sts. Fasten off.

Thumb

Sl 17 sts from holder back to needles, pick up 1 st on mitten edge, 2 sts over cast-on sts, 1 st on rem mitten edge—21 sts. Join, mark beg of rnd. Work in seed st, dec 2 sts on 1st rnd—19 sts. Work until thumb measures 2½"/6.5cm from beg, dec 1 st on last rnd—18 sts. **Next rnd** *K1, p2tog; rep from * around. Work 1 rnd even. **Next rnd** K2 tog around. Work 1 rnd even. Break yarn and fasten off as for mitten top.

LEFT MITTEN

Work to correspond to right mitten, reversing shaping and pattern placement.

women's cabled gloves

(Continued from page 110)

• St markers

• Safety pins

GAUGE

30 sts and 43 rows = 4"/10cm over seed st using larger needles. TAKE TIME TO CHECK GAUGE.

SEED STITCH (over any number of sts).

Row 1 (RS) *K1, p1; rep from * to end. **Row 2** K the purl sts and p the knit sts. Rep row 2 for seed st.

RIGHT GLOVE

With smaller needles, cast on 51 sts. **Row 1 (RS)** *K1, p1; rep from * end k1. **Row 2** *P1, k1; rep from * end p1. Rep these 2 rows for rib pat for 2"/5cm. Change to larger needles. Beg pat: **Row 1 (RS)** [P1, k1] 4 times; place marker (pm), p1, k3, sl 3 sts to cn and hold to front, k3, k3 from cn (6-st left cable-LC), p1, pm; [k1, p1] 16 times. **Row 2** [P1, k1] 16 times; k1, p9, k1; [k1, p1] 4 times. **Row 3** [P1, k1] 4 times; p1, sl 3 sts to cn and hold to back, k3, k3 from cn (6-st right cable-RC), k3, p1; [k1, p1] 16 times. **Row 4** Rep row 2. Work rows 1-4 for glove pat AT SAME TIME, work thumb gusset as foll: **Row 5** [P1, k1] 4 times; p1, k3, 6-st LC, p1; [k1, p1] 4 times, M1, k1, M1, work in seed st to end. Work 3 rows in pat. **Row 9** [P1, k1] 4 times; p1, k3, 6-st LC, p1; [k1, p1] 4 times, M1, p1, k1, p1, M1, work in seed st to end. Work 3 rows in pat. **Row 13** [P1, k1] 4 times; p1, k3, 6-st LC, p1; [k1, p1] 4 times, M1, [k1, p1] twice, k1, M1, work in seed st to end. Cont to inc in this way every 4th row, working incs into established seed st pat, until there are 63 sts. Work 3 more rows even in pat. **Beg thumb: Next row (RS)** Work 40 sts in pat, turn. Cast on 2 sts. **Next row** Work 15 sts in pat, turn. Cast on 2 sts. Work in seed st on these 17 sts (for thumb) for 2¼"/5.5cm, end with a WS row.

Top shaping

Next row (RS) [Work 1 st, work 2 sts tog] 5 times, work 2 sts tog—11 sts. Work 1 row even. **Next row** [Work 2 sts tog] 5 times, work 1 st. Cut yarn leaving an end for sewing. Draw through rem sts and pull tightly to fasten. Sew thumb seam. Return to sts for hand and from RS, rejoin yarn and work across sts, picking up 3 sts at base of thumb—53 sts. Work even for 1¼"/3cm, end with a WS row. **Next row (RS)** Work 6 sts, sl these sts to a safety pin for 4th finger. Cast on 1 st, work to last 6 sts, sl these sts to another safety pin for 4th finger. Cast on 1 st.

First finger

Next row (WS) Work 28 sts, turn. Cast on 1 st. **Next row** Work 15 sts, turn. Cast on 1 st. Work in seed st on these 16 sts (first finger) for 2¾"/7cm, end with a WS row. **Top Shaping: Next row (RS)** [Work 1 st, work 2 sts tog] 5 times, work 1 st. Work 1 row even. **Next row** [Work 2 sts tog] 5 times, work 1 st. Cut yarn and finish as for thumb.

Second finger

Working from RS, rejoin yarn at 7 sts before first finger, (front of hand), work these sts, pick up and k 2 sts at base of first finger; work next 7 sts, (back of hand), turn. Cast on 1 st. **Next row** Work 17 sts, turn. Cast on 1 st. Work in seed st on these 18 sts for 3¼"/8cm. **Top shaping: Next row (RS)** [Work 1 st, work 2 sts tog] 6 times. Work 1 row even. **Next row** [Work 2 sts tog] 6 times. Cut yarn and finish as for thumb.

Third finger

Rejoin yarn to sts after safety pin, and pick up and k 2 sts at base of second finger, work to sts before last safety pin. Cont as on first finger (on 15 sts) for 2¾"/7cm and finish as before.

Fourth finger

Working on sts from safety pins, pick up and k 2 sts at base of third finger. Work as before on 14 sts for 2¼"/5.5cm. **Next row (RS)** [Work 2 sts tog, work 1 st] 4 times, work 2 sts tog. Work 1 row even. **Next row** [Work 2 sts tog] 4 times, work 1 st. Finish as before.

LEFT GLOVE

Work wrist ribbing as for right glove. Change to larger needles. **Beg pat: Row 1 (RS)** [P1, k1] 16 times, p1, k3, 6-st LC, p1, [k1, p1] 4 times. Work in pat as set up for a total of 4 rows. Work thumb gusset as foll: **Row 5 (RS)** Seed st over first 23 sts, M1, k1, M1, work in pat to end. Cont as for right glove reversing shaping and placement of fingers as set up for left glove.

FINISHING

Carefully sew all seams so they remain flat. Wash gently and rinse with a softener, if desired. Lay flat to dry.

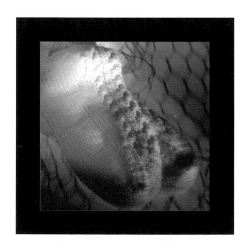

basic cable sock

(Continued from page 112)

* to end. Rep rows 1 and 2 until heel flap measures 2"/5cm, end with row 2.

Turn heel

Next row (WS) P16, p1, p2tog, turn. **Next row (RS)** Slip first st, k3, ssk, k1, turn. **Next row** Slip first st, p4, p2tog, p1, turn. Cont short rows in this way until all sts have been worked—18 sts rem.

Instep

With RS facing, pick up 13 sts along left edge of heel flap, work across 32 instep sts and transfer them to one needle, with the third needle, pick up 13 sts along the other edge of heel, work the next 9 sts of heel or to the center of the heel—76 sts (22 sts on needle 1, 32 sts on needle 2 and 22 sts on needle 3.

Note: Cont cable pat on top of sock only (32 sts of needle 2), work rem sts in St st. Join and cont to work in rnds as foll:

Instep shaping

Work 1 rnd even. **Next rnd** Work to last 3 sts of needle 1, k2tog, k1; work even across sts of needle 2; on needle 3, k1, ssk, work to end. Rep last 2 rnds until there are 58 sts. Work even in cable and St st as established until foot measures 7½"/19cm or 2"/5cm less than desired length, and on last rnd dec 6 sts evenly across 32 sts on needle 2. There are 13 sts on needles 1 and 3 and 26 sts on needle 2 for a total of 52 sts.

Toe shaping

Discontinue cable pattern and work all sts in St st as foll: Work 1 rnd even. **Next rnd** Work to last 3 sts of needle 1; k2tog, k1; at beg of needle 2 work k1, ssk, work to last 3 sts of same needle, k2tog, k1; at beg of needle 3 work k1, ssk, work to end of rnd. Rep last 2 rnds until there are 16 sts. Work to end of first needle and cut yarn, leaving an end for seaming. Place sts needles 1 and 3 onto one needle (8 sts on each of 2 needles) and weave sts tog using kitchener stitch.

argyle golf club covers

(Continued from page 114)

GAUGE

28 sts and 30 rows = 4"/10cm over cable rib (slightly stretched) using size 4 (3.5mm) needles.

TAKE TIME TO CHECK GAUGE.

CABLE RIB (multiple of 16 sts plus 3)

Rows 1 and 3 (WS) K1 (selvage st), k1, *p2, k2; rep from * to last st, k1 (selvage st). **Row 2** K1, p2, *k2, p2; rep from *, end p1, k1.

Row 4 K1, p2, *[k2, p2] twice, k2tog but do not drop sts from needle, insert RH needle between the 2 sts just knitted tog and k first st again, sl both sts from needle tog (cable made), p2, work cable over next 2 sts, p2; rep from *, end p1, k1. Rep rows 1-4 for cable rib.

COVERS

With size 4 (3.5mm) needles and MC, cast on 51 sts. Work in cable rib for 48 rows. P next row on WS, dec 3 sts evenly spaced across—48 sts. Discontinue selvage sts. Work 4 rows in St st. Work 23 rows chart pat. Cont with MC only to end of piece and work next row as foll: p 1 row on WS, dec 2 sts—46 sts.

Top shaping

Row 1 (RS) K2, [k4, k2tog] 7 times, k2—39 sts. **Row 2 and all WS rows** Purl. **Row 3** K2, [k3, k2tog] 7 times, k2—32 sts. **Row 5** K2, [k2, k2tog] 7 times, k2—25 sts. **Row 7** K2, [k1, k2tog] 7 times, k2—18 sts. Cut yarn, leaving an end for sewing.

FINISHING

Pull end through rem sts and sew back seam.

Pompoms

Make six 1½"/4cm diameter pompons as foll: 2 each in colors A, B and C. Sew one of each color to top of cover.

Color Key

☐ White (MC)

⊡ Navy (A)

⊠ Red (B)

◪ Green (C)

23
20
10
1

└─ 12-st rep ─┘

gingham golf club covers

(Continued from page 114)

p1, sl 1 wyif, *p2, sl 2 wyif; rep from *, end p2, sl 1 wyif, p1. **Row 4** With A, knit. **Row 5** With C, p2, *sl 2 wyif, p2; rep from * to end. **Row 6** With C, k2, *sl 2 wyib, k2; rep from * to end. Rep rows 1-6 for check pat.

COVERS

With size 4 (3.5mm) needles and MC, cast on 54 sts. Work in k2, p2 rib for 6"/15cm, end with a RS row. Work in check pat for 47 rows.

Top shaping

Next row (RS) With C, k2, [sl 2 wyib, k2tog, sl 2 wyib, k2] 6 times, sl 2 wyib, k2—48 sts. **Next row** With A, purl. **Next row** With B, k1, sl 1 wyib, [k1, sl 1 wyib, k2tog, sl 2 wyib] 7 times, k2, sl 1 wyib, k1—41 sts. **Next row** With B, p1, sl 1 wyif, [p2tog, sl 2 wyif, p2, sl 1 wyif] 5 times, p2, sl 1 wyif, p1—36 sts. Cont with A only to end of piece as foll: K next row, working k2tog over each pair of B sts—30 sts. P 1 row. **Next row** [K1, k2tog] 10 times—20 sts. P 1 row. **Next row** K2tog across—10 sts. Cut yarn, leaving an end for sewing.

FINISHING

Pull end through rem sts and sew back seam.

Pompoms

Make a 3"/7.5cm diameter pompon with B and sew to top of cover.

resources

Artisan NZ
distributed by
Cherry Tree Hill Yarns

Baabajoes Wool Company
PO Box 260604
Lakewood, CO 80226
www.baabajoeswool.com

Blue Sky Alpacas
PO Box 387
St. Francis, MN 55070

Berroco, Inc.
14 Elmdale Road
PO Box 367
Uxbridge, MA 01569

Brown Sheep Yarn Company
100662 County Road 16
Mitchell, NE 69357

Cherry Tree Hill Yarn
PO Box 659
Barton, VT 05822

Classic Elite Yarns
300A Jackson Ave.
Lowell, MA 01854
www.classiceliteyarns.com

Crystal Palace
2340 Bissell Avenue
Richmond, CA 94804
www.straw.com

Colinette Yarns
distributed by
Unique Kolours

Colorado Yarns
PO Box 217
Colorado Springs, CO 80903

Dale of Norway, Inc.
N16 W23390 Stoneridge Drive
Suite A
Waukesha, WI 53188

Debbie Bliss
distributed by
Knitting Fever, Inc.

Fiesta Yarns
4583 Corrales Road
Corrales, NM 87048

Filatura Di Crosa
distributed by
Tahki•Stacy Charles, Inc.

GGH
distributed by
Muench Yarns

Indiecita
distributed by
Plymouth Yarns

JCA
35 Scales Lane
Townsend, MA 01469

Jaeger Handknits
4 Townsend West, Unit 8
Nashua, NH

Jilly Knitwear
PO Box 26053
London SW109GX
England
Info@jillyknitwear.com

Knit One Crochet Too
7 Commons Ave., Suite 2
Windham, ME 04062

Knitting Fever, Inc.
P. O. Box 502
Roosevelt, NY 11575

Koigu Wool Designs
RR #1
Williamsford, ON N0H 2V0
Canada
koigu@hotmail.com

Lana Gatto
distributed by
Needful Yarns, Inc.

La Lana Wools
136 Paseo Norte
Taos, NM 87571

Les Fils Muench
5640 Rue Valcourt
Brossard, PQ J4W 1C5
Canada

Mango Moon
412 N. Coast Hwy #114
Laguna Beach, CA 92651

Muench Yarns
285 Bel Marin Keys Blvd.
Unit J
Novato, CA 94949-5724

Needful Yarns, Inc.
4476 Chesswood Drive
Suite 10 & 11
Toronto, ON M3J 2B9
(866) 800-4700

Noro
distributed by
Knitting Fever, Inc.

Patons®
PO Box 40
Listowel, ON N4W 3H3
Canada
www.patonsyarns.com

Plymouth Yarn
PO Box 28
Bristol, PA 19007

Reynolds
distributed by
JCA

Schoeller Stahl
distributed by
Skacel Collection

Skacel Collection
PO Box 88110
Seattle, WA 98138-2110
(800) 255-1278

Tahki Yarns
distributed by
Tahki•Stacy Charles, Inc.

Tahki•Stacy Charles, Inc.
8000 Cooper Ave., Bldg. 1
Glendale, NY 11385
(800) 338-YARN
tahki@worldnet.att.net

Trendsetter Yarns
16742 Stagg Street
Suite 104
Van Nuys, CA 91406

Unique Kolours
28 North Bacton Hill Road
Malvern, PA 19355
(800) 252-3934

Wendy
distributed by
Berroco, Inc.

Wool Pak Yarns NZ
distributed by
Baabajoes Wool Company

We have made every effort to ensure the accuracy of the contents of this publication. We are not responsible for any human or typographical errors.